SALVATION

Strait & Narrow

Mark Q. Bullen

Salvation – Strait & Narrow

ISBN-13: 978-0692394311
ISBN-10: 0692394311

Apprehending Truth Publishers
PO Box 249
Brookfield, Missouri 64628

AT 10 9 8 7 6 5 4
170121

Living Faith Books is an imprint of:
Apprehending Truth Publishers
PO Box 249
Brookfield, Missouri 64628
http://www.atpublishers.com

Also by Mark Q. Bullen

What The Bible Really Teaches About Divorce and Remarriage

Did Jesus Correct Moses?

God's Crucible: Life in a Biblical Church

The Alien Exposed: An Acid Test for the Authentic Anabaptist
Love of Truth

Resist Not Evil???

Salvation – Strait and Narrow (*Audiobook*)

Living Faith Books

Apprehending Truth Publishers
Brookfield, Missouri

CONTENTS

Chapter One

The Purpose and Power of Parables

When I say "prodigal son", what comes to your mind? If I say "good Samaritan" what comes to your mind? Do you realize how many principles and truths are compressed into those short stories? If a picture is worth a thousand words, then a parable of Christ is worth a thousand theologians. Erroneous views about salvation are often built on isolated verses from discourses either doctrinal or prophetic; and their proponents usually avoid the parables of Jesus. The parables are too plain and understandable. They make too much sense! You cannot get the crazy ideas of false teachings from the parables, because they are connected to the common sense of everyday life on earth that we understand. God's Word and ways are very practical and reasonable. If we would listen closer to the parables, we would grasp the concepts of salvation and Christ's Kingdom much better.

The reason Jesus often taught with parables is because of the power of parables to fix an image in our minds. The image is something we are familiar with and illustrates spiritual truths that otherwise may be hard to understand. Farmers can all comprehend the dynamics in the "Parable of the Sower" (Luke 8). When these agricultural principles are then applied to the dynamics of evangelism and salvation; they are much more easily

1

assimilated by the seeker of truth. Spiritual ideas left in the abstract might be hard to "picture"; but in the parable we can "see" it. In this way Jesus proved that God's dealings with man are based on principles that can be illustrated through our earthly experiences, and are thus **reasonable** to our finite minds. They are not so far out and mystical that we cannot grasp them as reasonable, just, righteous and wise.

When somebody tells you of something God supposedly does that seems very unreasonable, illogical, or unjust, like the five points of Calvinism; and then they justify it by simply saying, *"His ways are not our ways";* you can be fairly certain they really don't know what they are talking about. God's ways are indeed above our ways in that they are based on pure, holy, and just motives; but they are not above our ability to see, admire, and learn from their reasonableness, wisdom, and superiority. God is infinitely greater than we are; and I'm sure there are concepts and knowledge too wonderful for us to even imagine; but I'm speaking of God's dealings with man. I'm speaking about God reaching out to communicate and save man. I'm speaking of what God has revealed of himself in His Holy Word. God's revelation of himself was not meant to appear unreasonable and illogical; but to appeal to our understanding and win our admiration.

We are supposed to be emulating and learning God's ways, which proves they are based on principles we can comprehend and be thus led to worship our wise, just, and loving God. Did not God create us in His own image so we could worship and admire Him and His ways? Fathers should seek to be fathers like Him. Governors should seek to govern like Him. God's governmental principles by which He governs the universe are to be our patterns for all earthly government (Re 15:3,4). He is the "Just One", and is striving to lead us to be partakers of His divine nature. Listen to God's clear reasoning with man concerning the rightness of God's ways compared with the false concepts of man in Ezekiel 18. Does God think we should be able to understand His ways?

Ez 18:1 ¶ *The word of the LORD came unto me again, saying,*
2 What mean ye, that ye use this proverb concerning the land of Israel, saying, The fathers have eaten sour grapes, and the children's teeth are set on edge?
3 As I live, saith the Lord GOD, ye shall not have occasion any more to use this proverb in Israel.
4 Behold, all souls are mine; as the soul of the father, so also the soul of the son is mine: the soul that sinneth, it shall die.
5 But if a man be just, and do that which is lawful and right,
...9 Hath walked in my statutes, and hath kept my judgments, to deal truly; he is just, he shall surely live, saith the Lord GOD.
10 ¶ If he beget a son that is a robber, a shedder of blood, and that doeth the like to any one of these things,
...shall he then live? he shall not live: he hath done all these abominations; he shall surely die; his blood shall be upon him.
14 Now, lo, if he beget a son, that seeth all his father's sins which he hath done, and considereth, and doeth not such like,...but hath given his bread to the hungry, and hath covered the naked with a garment,
17 That hath taken off his hand from the poor, that hath not received usury nor increase, hath executed my judgments, hath walked in my statutes; he shall not die for the iniquity of his father, he shall surely live.
18 As for his father, because he cruelly oppressed, spoiled his brother by violence, and did that which is not good among his people, lo, even he shall die in his iniquity.
19 Yet say ye, Why? doth not the son bear the iniquity of the father? When the son hath done that which is lawful and right, and hath kept all my statutes, and hath done them, he shall surely live.

3

20 The soul that sinneth, it shall die. The son shall not bear the iniquity of the father, neither shall the father bear the iniquity of the son: the righteousness of the righteous shall be upon him, and the wickedness of the wicked shall be upon him.

21 ¶ But if the wicked will turn from all his sins that he hath committed, and keep all my statutes, and do that which is lawful and right, he shall surely live, he shall not die.

22 All his transgressions that he hath committed, they shall not be mentioned unto him: in his righteousness that he hath done he shall live.

23 Have I any pleasure at all that the wicked should die? saith the Lord GOD: and not that he should return from his ways, and live?

24 But when the righteous turneth away from his righteousness, and committeth iniquity, and doeth according to all the abominations that the wicked man doeth, shall he live? All his righteousness that he hath done shall not be mentioned: in his trespass that he hath trespassed, and in his sin that he hath sinned, in them shall he die.

25 Yet ye say, The way of the Lord is not equal. Hear now, O house of Israel; Is not my way equal? are not your ways unequal?

26 When a righteous man turneth away from his righteousness, and committeth iniquity, and dieth in them; for his iniquity that he hath done shall he die.

27 Again, when the wicked man turneth away from his wickedness that he hath committed, and doeth that which is lawful and right, he shall save his soul alive.

28 Because he considereth, and turneth away from all his transgressions that he hath committed, he shall surely live, he shall not die.

*29 Yet saith the house of Israel, The way of the Lord is not equal. O house of Israel, **are not my ways equal? are not your ways unequal?***

*30 ¶ Therefore I will judge you, O house of Israel, every one according to his ways, saith the Lord GOD. **Repent, and turn yourselves from all your transgressions; so iniquity shall not be your ruin.***

31 Cast away from you all your transgressions, whereby ye have transgressed; and make you a new heart and a new spirit: for why will ye die, O house of Israel?
32 For I have no pleasure in the death of him that dieth, saith the Lord GOD: wherefore turn yourselves, and live ye.

They accused God of having unjust ways, but God explains the common sense justice of His ways, and tells them that it is their ways that are unjust and inconsistent. Again in Ezekiel 33 God tries to reason with Israel that His ways were rational, understandable, and reasonable according to right concepts of justice and equity that any unbiased mind should be able to comprehend. If God didn't expect people to understand and appreciate the logic and reasonableness of His ways, why would He waste time reasoning with them? Listen closely to God's Gospel message of repentance, grace, pardon, and new birth with a new heart and spirit. These are the foundation stones for the same concepts in the New Testament; which is why Jesus expected Nicodemus to understand what He was saying.

Ez 33:11 *Say unto them, As I live, saith the Lord GOD, I have no pleasure in the death of the wicked; but that the wicked turn from his way and live: turn ye, turn ye from your evil ways; for why will ye die, O house of Israel?*
12 Therefore, thou son of man, say unto the children of thy people, The righteousness of the righteous shall not deliver him in the day of his transgression: as for the wickedness of the wicked, he shall not fall thereby in the day that he turneth from his wickedness; neither shall the righteous be able to live for his righteousness in the day that he sinneth.
13 When I shall say to the righteous, that he shall surely live; if he trust to his own righteousness, and commit iniquity, all his righteousnesses shall not be remembered; but for his iniquity that he hath committed, he shall die for it.

14 Again, when I say unto the wicked, Thou shalt surely die; if he turn from his sin, and do that which is lawful and right;

15 If the wicked restore the pledge, give again that he had robbed, walk in the statutes of life, without committing iniquity; he shall surely live, he shall not die.

16 None of his sins that he hath committed shall be mentioned unto him: he hath done that which is lawful and right; he shall surely live.

17 Yet the children of thy people say, **The way of the Lord is not equal: but as for them, their way is not equal.**

18 When the righteous turneth from his righteousness, and committeth iniquity, he shall even die thereby.

19 But if the wicked turn from his wickedness, and do that which is lawful and right, he shall live thereby.

20 **Yet ye say, The way of the Lord is not equal.** *O ye house of Israel, I will judge you every one after his ways.*

God is preaching the Gospel to Israel. God's judgments deal with the pardon or damnation of the soul, not just the natural consequences of our foolish choices in this life. God allowing trouble in this life is a merciful attempt to get our attention and lead us to repentance (Rom 2:4). God's ways are reasonable and just to the thinking man; and we should glean divine wisdom from His ways and apply them in our own judgments. Being that God's just and righteous governmental principles are logical and reasonable to the judicious mind; we can clearly see how parables can effectively illustrate and teach God's ways. God presents himself as a loving Father; and Jesus presents himself as a faithful, obedient son. Why? Because everyone on earth can grasp the beauty of such a relationship and learn from it. Jesus is presented as a king, a husbandman, a shepherd, a physician, a prophet, a husband, a priest, and a faithful son or prince. In all these roles He illustrates principles of God's relationship with man, and we can learn through them what is expected of us, and also what we can expect of God.

All the false concepts of grace, faith, justification, salvation, and love could easily be overcome if men would simply listen to Christ's parables and stop trying to make these principles so mystical and incomprehensible. If we would use the same common sense with heavenly concepts as we do with similar earthly circumstances, we would understand God's Word much better. If we saw a parent exercising the same false "grace" with a disobedient child that men expect from God, we would say they are a foolish parent just spoiling the child and creating a monster. We would easily understand their "grace" to be "lasciviousness", and not true appropriate grace (Jude 4). Any parent, who just automatically forgave a child, while that child continued disobeying, would be despised by anyone concerned about the child's future and his impact on society. People need to get their religion and common sense back in the same cranial cavity, and stop presenting God's ways to the world in such a fashion as destroys right concepts of justice, mercy, love, and grace.

When Jesus taught God's ways, they made such sense as to silence his adversaries. His parables appealed directly to their own sense of justice and righteousness. Jesus gave the parable of a king who took account of his servants. One was brought forward who owed him an immense sum of ten thousand talents. What happened?

Mt 18:25 *But forasmuch as he had not to pay, his lord commanded him to be sold, and his wife, and children, and all that he had, and payment to be made.*

26 The servant therefore fell down, and worshipped him, saying, Lord, have patience with me, and I will pay thee all.

27 Then the lord of that servant was moved with compassion, and loosed him, and forgave him the debt.

28 But the same servant went out, and found one of his fellowservants, which owed him an hundred pence: and he laid hands on him, and took him by the throat, saying, Pay me that thou owest.

29 And his fellowservant fell down at his feet, and besought him, saying, Have patience with me, and I will pay thee all.

30 And he would not: but went and cast him into prison, till he should pay the debt.

31 So when his fellowservants saw what was done, they were very sorry, and came and told unto their lord all that was done.

32 Then his lord, after that he had called him, said unto him, O thou wicked servant, I forgave thee all that debt, because thou desiredst me:

33 Shouldest not thou also have had compassion on thy fellowservant, even as I had pity on thee?

34 And his lord was wroth, and delivered him to the tormentors, till he should pay all that was due unto him.

*35 **So likewise shall my heavenly Father do also unto you,** if ye from your hearts forgive not every one his brother their trespasses."*

Now, anyone with an unbiased mind can clearly see the ways of the Lord here are understandable and logical. The man with the great debt was forgiven by the king's grace when he fell down and begged mercy because he could not pay the debt. This man then went out and failed to show the same compassion on his fellow servant who owed him just a small amount in comparison to his great debt. When the king saw this, he was very unhappy and...did what?? **He revoked the forgiveness already given, and made the man pay his debt.** Would God revoke my forgiveness because I failed to forgive a fellow servant who besought me to have compassion on him?

Jesus said so. This is very understandable; but also shoots holes in many false doctrines like "once saved always saved", etc. **The King only had grace when it was appropriate; but not when it ceased to be appropriate.**

Jesus gave the Parable of the Sower, which teaches many wonderful and clear truths about life and salvation. The main idea is that if the Word of God falls on uncultivated, stony, or weedy soil it will not bring forth fruit to completion; which makes it worthless to the husbandman. Some will grow for a while, but then wither and die when the going gets tough. Some will grow, but be choked and distracted due to weeds (other competing plants), and never bring any fruit to maturity. Only the plant from the seed that falls on good ground and brings forth the fruit desired by God will be accepted of Him (See John 15 & Hebrews 6). This fruit is clearly said to be the keeping of His Word through patient obedience. Let God be true, but every theologian a liar.

The Parable of the wise and foolish virgins makes it quite clear that those who are not ready when the Lord returns will not be accepted, no matter how ready they may have been earlier. The Parables about the talents and the pounds speak to the same end, i.e. that if we have not been doing what we should, and are not prepared to meet the Lord, then we will be cast out and given our portion with the unbelievers. Our Lord's parables put spiritual realities in an easy to understand format that cannot be missed by the unbiased mind. Notwithstanding all this, men still confuse and cloud the obvious and plain teachings of the Lord to defend some peculiar prejudice they have.

Some will say that the parables were said to conceal the truth rather than reveal it (Mt 13:1-13). Did Jesus say that parables were to hide truth rather than explain it? No, that is not what He said. He said that he speaks parables to the people who have no desire to search further, rather than casting the pearls of truth before hard hearts, deaf ears, and blind eyes which refuse to see. By simply giving out the parable to the crowd and saving the interpretation for the seekers who asked further, He weeded out those who had not ears to hear. Only the disciples who followed and inquired received the gold nuggets of truth. The parables were not meant to hide truth; but when placed with the interpretation, they were meant to make truth compatible to our understanding – to present heavenly realities in an earthly format. We, who have a Bible, have not only the parables, but also the interpretations.

God's ways can be clearly seen in the reflection of earthly matters and issues we face. God's grace, love, and mercy fit perfectly with what we would expect from a godly father, governor, shepherd, or king. There is NO CONFLICT between justice and righteousness in earthly matters of government and heavenly matters. Therefore we can know that if it is just to do something on earth, then it is ALSO God's way of doing it. We can illustrate the doctrines of salvation through earthly parables like Jesus did and thus help people to picture doctrinal concepts. If people can picture these doctrinal concepts in action, they usually will not miss or distort God's message. Heresies such at "unconditional eternal security", "Calvinism", "easy believism", "false grace", etc. will not fit in earthly models, because they would not make sense. Earthly kings, shepherds, physicians, etc.

could not operate with these false concepts because they make no sense, are unjust, unsustainable, and lead to foolishness. God's ways, on the other hand, can ALL be illustrated by just and righteous human affairs; and are the very patterns we should follow.

Now that we have hopefully established this point in your mind and heart; I wish to follow Christ's wise and effective example to answer some widespread errors that have stumbled thousands of seeking souls. In the format of two basic parables about God's salvation program, I hope to make some concepts clear that Satan has worked to confuse and change. If you listen close, I believe you will gain some insights and answers for those who are confused about these important matters. If you will open your eyes and heart, you should be able to SEE Biblical principles and doctrinal concepts clearer and more accurate than before. I want you to be able to see the mechanics of God's salvation program in action so they make sense to your mind.

Chapter Two

Parable of The Gracious King

Once there was a great King with many subjects. There was one class of subjects for whom he had shown special favors, and provided them with a nice living in a beautiful section of his country. The King's enemy, knowing the care that the King had for these subjects, went and lied to the heads of this people and told them the King's kindness was just to selfishly keep them under his rule; because the King knew they were such a great people they could do better without him. The heads of this people believed this enemy and rebelled against the King; - who in consequence banished them from his domain and annulled their citizenship.

Immediately the people could see they had made a grave mistake and petitioned the king accordingly, who said they must live out their banishment and learn well their lesson until a program could be devised to restore them; but this he promised to do. He also promised that after this he would execute judgment on the enemy that deceived them, and destroy those who sided with him. As time went on and the enemy of the King continued to tell them lies about the King, many, who couldn't remember what it was like in the King's domain, believed the enemy that they were indeed better off than before, and valued their personal liberty to be their own lord more than the blessing of living in the King's domain.

What they didn't realize was that this enemy was now their king, which was his whole design from the start.

The Great King, knowing these people were headed for destruction, seeing their miserable condition, and knowing that they were better off by far under his government; devised a gracious and merciful plan to save and restore all who really wanted to be back under his government. These people, however, were now naturally dangerous to his realm since they had been so indoctrinated by his enemy and trained in selfishness. He knew there would have to be a special program to convert them back to his way of thinking, train them in proper respect and obedience to his holy laws, and restore their confidence in his government.

He set up clinics in their district that would teach true and right principles of government and also tell of how well people could live under the rule of a just and righteous king. He sent ambassadors to proclaim his offer of mercy to any who would comply with his terms and reconcile with his government. Anyone who would listen to the king's decrees and desire his offered rehabilitation were initiated into the king's program: They had to renounce their former indoctrination and the kings' enemy, profess that they were guilty of treason and rebellion against their rightful lord, profess that they were now returning to his lordship, and that they desired to be fully trained in the principles of his government. These people were then given a badge to wear declaring they were now subjects of the Great King, and were living by his laws under his government once again. The badge was a token from the king declaring that, if they continued in their training and were found faithful, they would be restored to the king's domain to live in his presence with full privileges as faithful sons and daughters of the king. The enemy hated this and began trying to kill or discredit those who were sent from the king and persecute those who wore the badges.

The wise king knew that for them to wear this badge amongst the rebels in that realm would be a good test of their sincerity; weed out the insincere; and expose those who really did not have full confidence in the king's government. The wise king knew they would suffer persecution for returning to him, their rightful lord, while living in the enemy's territory. If they would wear this badge and faithfully train at the clinics for a specified number of months, enduring whatever trouble they suffered as a result, they could then be restored to the King's domain and live with full citizenship in the presence of the king as before they fell.

This was a covenant relationship that the Great King set up; and his own faithful son, who had himself paid the ransom price for the necessary legal atonement, was set up as the administrator of the covenant. He was the High Priest of the covenant, and whenever there was a breach of the covenant – no matter how small – the people who were badge wearing trainees would have to apply to the king's son to intercede for them to the king to refresh their pardon, and cleanse their record of trespass. This grace wasn't obligatory upon the king, or his son, and the people had to be careful lest they offend the king so as to be cut off from the covenant. The king, however, that cared enough to devise the plan surely would be patient and gracious to any sincere and striving applicant who was really desiring to learn; and not just presuming upon his grace and thus seeking to enter the king's domain without true heart repentance and love for the king and his son. The clinic officers continually reminded the trainees how important it was for them to convince the king of their sincerity, love, and faithfulness. The king's final acceptance was dependent upon them convincing him that they really agreed with him, his ways, his government, and truly desired him to rule over them again. They were to convince the king during this time of testing that they wanted his government over them, would be faithful subjects, and would not be an embarrassment to the king's son who paid for their redemption.

The enemy of the king, naturally desiring to defeat this purpose, keep the people under his control, and bring reproach upon the king's son; set up false clinics and told more lies concerning the king. One false clinic began telling men that, since the king claimed his program was out of sincere grace, mercy and love, then all you had to do was be initiated – sign the proper documents and receive the badge – even if you just hid it in your pocket. They also taught you didn't have to train, be taught the king's ways, live by his laws, or attend the training sessions at the clinic; but could live as your own king still; and yet, just because you had the badge in your pocket, you would be restored and live in the king's realm. They went so far as to say, that even if you lost or threw away the badge, just because you received it at the beginning, you would still be accepted. They declared that since the badge was a token of the king's acceptance, if the king now didn't accept you, he was a liar. If he had promised to receive those who were given the badge and then didn't receive them, he wasn't being truthful. What they didn't tell was that the badges the false clinics handed out didn't come from the king, but were counterfeits. They also didn't tell that the badge was originally meant to be a token of acceptance into the covenant rehabilitation program, not final acceptance into the king's realm. The faithful, whole-hearted keeping of the king's covenant to the end of the program is what the king demanded before they could be finally accepted into the king's realm. Numerous false clinics and much misinformation was spread by the enemy; but the simple, common sense program of the king was the only path to restoration; and graduation from the king's program was the only graduation that would give access to the king's domain. All the other misled trainees would be rejected and left under the enemy's rule to be destroyed with him.

The Great King allowed all this because ultimately it served his interests in sifting and proving the hearts of the repentant. Those who were deceived and led astray by the enemy's false clinics were so led due to inner preferences in their own hearts. If they loved the king's ways, they would naturally prefer the king's clinics and avoid the false clinics. Thus the wise king harvested the genuinely repentant people who would make loyal subjects and never jeopardize his son's honor.

We could go on and on – but we have laid this foundation for a purpose.

Chapter Three

Kingdom Considerations

If the King demanded full repentance and a return to whole hearted obedience – does that make his program and promised salvation anything less than a gift or of grace? No, not in the slightest. Meeting the conditions of the program **in no way paid for the program**, **in no way helped pay the ransom paid by the king's son**, and **in no way paid the king for his gracious plan.** The whole program was still a free gift of mercy and grace from the KING. Anyone with common sense ought to be able to see this.

The people committed treason and were banished because they believed the enemy, and not the king. Their whole restoration was then rightly centered around them showing they had changed their minds; now believed the king; and now counted the enemy as a liar. But how would they show this? How would the king know they were genuine and sincere? They would be judged by their **works** – Nothing reveals the genuineness of faith, like our deeds do. What we actually **do** is the ultimate test of our **"want to"**. The Bible clearly says we will be judged by our works, but never says we will be judged by our faith, love, etc. O yes, we will be judged in these areas, but God wisely knows to judge these issues by our **works**. Jesus said, He that hath my commandments and keepeth them, he it is that loveth me. Our love and faith can only be judged by our works. The king would look at the works and declare either, "that person believes me" or "that person doesn't believe me". The heart is deceitful; and millions believe they have a "good heart" while they actually hate God's government and would dethrone Him if they had the power. How do I know? I know, because they dethrone Him daily in their choices and works where they presently have the power to do so. God sees this and knows they hate Him, though deceived in their heart that they love Him. God sees their deeds! Their daily choices vote for who they want as their king.

What "**works**" then was the king looking for? Well, obviously he wanted to see a repentant heart and a changed mind. They would reveal this in seeking to please the king, joining the clinic by the prescribed initiation, wearing the badge, and living in accord with all that was taught at the king's clinics. The clinic officers would clearly be able to discern by the spirit and attitude of every trainee. Those who were truly repentant and grateful would naturally show a humble enthusiasm for what the King's clinics were trying to accomplish.

We have the same conditions upon us that we find in this parable. God, our gracious King, expects genuine repentance, baptism, faithful church membership, and a fervent holy life in an effort to please God and learn His ways. Wouldn't this make sense? Listen to what our King's clinic officers have said as they even quote the words of the King Himself:

2 Co 6:14 *Be ye not unequally yoked together with unbelievers: for what fellowship hath righteousness with unrighteousness? and what communion hath light with darkness? 15 And what concord hath Christ with Belial? or what part hath he that believeth with an infidel? 16 And what agreement hath the temple of God with idols? for ye are the temple of the living God; as God hath said, I will dwell in them, and walk in them; and I will be their God, and they shall be my people. 17* **Wherefore come out from among them, and be ye separate, saith the Lord, and touch not the unclean thing; and I will receive you, 18 And will be a Father unto you, and ye shall be my sons and daughters, saith the Lord Almighty.**

What does the apostle Paul say in response to this conditional covenant relationship? In the very next verse, Paul says:

2 Co 7:1 ¶ **Having** *therefore these promises, dearly beloved,* **let us** *cleanse ourselves from all filthiness of the flesh and spirit, perfecting holiness in the fear of God.*

Having this present conditional relationship, let us meet the conditions! (See Ro. 8:13 and I Jn 1:7-9) If the King heard that there was a man or woman who did not like attending the clinic training, and was not eager to learn; what would the King naturally conclude? Do you think He would want this person reinstated as a citizen of His Kingdom? Do you think the King would want this ungrateful and unrepentant person to reap the benefits of His Son's great sacrifice? You know He would not. What does our King say about such things?

Heb 10:21 *And having an high priest over the house of God; 22 Let us draw near with a true heart in full assurance of faith, having our hearts sprinkled from an evil conscience, and our bodies washed with pure water. 23 Let us hold fast the profession of our faith without wavering; (for he is faithful that promised;) 24 And let us consider one another to provoke unto love and to good works:* **25 Not forsaking the assembling of ourselves together, as the manner of some is;** *but exhorting* *one another: and so much the more, as ye see the day approaching. 26 For **if we sin wilfully after that we have received the knowledge of the truth, there remaineth no more sacrifice for sins, 27 But a certain fearful looking for of judgment and fiery indignation, which shall devour the adversaries.***

Does it have to get any clearer? Our King will not accept a person who is not whole heartedly repentant and grateful; but rather He sees them as an enemy of His gracious government. Either you are enthusiastic about fulfilling God's program, or you are a subtle enemy of God's program. This is clearly seen by what you do and what you support.

What would this king in our story think if he heard that one of the clinic trainees was not showing due respect to the clinic officers or the decrees of the king?   How does our King see this?

Heb 13:17 *Obey them that have the rule over you, and submit yourselves: for they watch for your souls, as they that must give account, that they may do it with joy, and not with grief: for that is unprofitable for you.*

What if a trainee was presumptuous and thought he knew better what would save more people than what the king had prescribed? What would it mean if he was more concerned about "saving souls" than meeting the king's requirements to save souls? Wouldn't this communicate that he was more concerned about people getting the benefits of the king's realm than he was about the kings' honor and goals? Would this not tell the king that this man had motives which put the rightness of the king's demands as a lower priority while putting the welfare of his friends as the first priority? Would not this man be dangerous to the government of the king? If this man was pushing his own agenda without truly being repentant and submitted to the king; then he was nothing more than a usurper who would dethrone the king and set himself up if he had the power. His real desire was to become popular by bettering himself and his friends at the king's expense. He was, at the same time, diminishing their crimes, their danger to the king's righteous government, and the need for them to repent and be completely changed before they could be safely reinstated as citizens of the king's realm. Can you see the conflict of interest here?

All who think the kings' first priority should be saving the lost, miss the point that the safety and honor of the King's righteous law and government is a higher priority; which is why the people were banished in the first place. Saving the lost must be done without compromising the King's law or government. The very reason they are lost or banished is because the King would not compromise His righteousness for them. The only way they can be restored is to eliminate the danger they pose to righteousness. They must convince the King of the genuineness of their repentance and change of mind. They must show that they love the King's laws and desire to uphold and promote his righteous government. Did the apostles of Christ deal with such dynamics? Most definitely.

Ro 10:3 *For they being ignorant of God's righteousness, and going about to establish their own righteousness, have not submitted themselves unto the righteousness of God.*

Php 2:21 *For all seek their own, not the things which are Jesus Christ's.*

23

2Co 11:2 For I am jealous over you with godly jealousy: for I have espoused you to one husband, that I may present you as a chaste virgin to Christ. 3 But I fear, lest by any means, as the serpent beguiled Eve through his subtilty, so your minds should be corrupted from the simplicity that is in Christ. 4 For if he that cometh preacheth another Jesus, whom we have not preached, or if ye receive another spirit, which ye have not received, or another gospel, which ye have not accepted, ye might well bear with him.

Then what? Obviously what happened to Eve would happen to them – they would fall and be rejected. It is vitally important that we prove to God our loyalty to His Son Jesus Christ, lest we be counted a danger to His righteous kingdom and be cast out.

Mt 10:37 He that loveth father or mother more than me is not worthy of me: and he that loveth son or daughter more than me is not worthy of me. 38 And he that taketh not his cross, and followeth after me, is not worthy of me.

Mk 8:38 Whosoever therefore shall be ashamed of me and of my words in this adulterous and sinful generation; of him also shall the Son of man be ashamed, when he cometh in the glory of his Father with the holy angels.

The Term "Salvation" includes the entire process required to bring a lost man to the resurrection of the just; but there are definite terms for the different steps of the process. You need to understand these terms.

Atonement is the price paid to make the pardon a legal transaction. Jesus is the only one who could pay the ransom price to satisfy God's holy law. God never cuts corners on principles of law and righteousness, not even when it costs Him dearly. In order for God to lay aside the execution of the law and pardon a repentant sinner, there had to be a sufficient price paid to satisfy the demands of righteous law and order in God's government. (See Chap. 10)

Justification is the process whereby the atonement is applied to the individual's legal standing before the King and His court. It is the actual cleansing of your record before God. God graciously wipes your sin list clean. In doing this He automatically imputes righteousness to you; because that is what a clean record declares. Though you have not earned this declaration of righteous deeds done (the clean record); yet God imputes your faith (seen in genuine repentance) to you for righteousness by wiping your record clean and granting you a pardon. Jesus' good deeds were not put on your record as some erroneously teach; but the simple cleansing of your record from trespasses is that which gives you a righteous standing before God. This clean record must be maintained through Jesus, your High Priest. Listen closely to the following verses as I give the proper verb tenses from the Greek:

Heb 7:24 *But this man (Jesus), because he continueth ever, hath an unchangeable priesthood. 25 Wherefore he is able also to save them to the uttermost that come **(continually come)** unto God by him, seeing he ever liveth to make intercession for them.*

Jesus is your High Priest ministering in the tabernacle of heaven with his own blood on our behalf; but we must continually come and confess sins to Him to keep our record clean. Obviously we can only confess the sins we know; but as we walk in all the light we have been given, He continually cleanses us from even those trespasses we are unaware of.

I Jn 1:6 *If we say that we have fellowship with him, and walk in darkness, we lie, and do not the truth: 7 But **if we walk in the light,** as he is in the light, we have fellowship one with another, and the blood of Jesus Christ his Son **(continually) cleanseth us from all sin.** 8 If we say that we have no sin, we deceive ourselves, and the truth is not in us. 9 **If we confess our sins,** he is faithful and just to forgive us our sins, and to cleanse us from all unrighteousness.*

This is the work of our high priest to maintain our justified state before God. As anyone can see, we have a part to play in this. We must walk in the light, and confess known sins to our high priest to maintain our clean record before God. That we have a part to play in no way makes the work of our High Priest any less a gift of grace. We are simply meeting conditions of eligibility to partake of His free grace; we are not earning or paying for anything. If I offered a free gallon of milk from our dairy to anyone over 18 who showed up between 8AM and 10AM Tuesday morning; would meeting those conditions make the free gallon of milk any less free?   Meeting the conditions of the free gift and paying for the milk are two very different things.

Reconciliation is the goal of all God's gracious provisions of salvation. It is a reuniting of man with his God on terms a Holy God can comply with.   God through Christ paved a legal way for man to reconcile with his rightful Lord and King. Being that the King was never in the wrong, all the "moving", "changing", and "re-aligning" must be on man's part. God, the King of Kings, will not meet man in the middle or negotiate for terms of peace. He was right, and He will not depart from His righteous position. He has been infinitely offended and wickedly trespassed against. It is only the amazing grace of His benevolent heart that moves him to make a strait and narrow path that leads to reconciliation – a return to his favor and care. Any attitude toward the demands of this narrow path other than humble grateful enthusiasm is simply rebellion remaining in the heart against the King and His righteous government.

Predestination is a term referring to God's plan and program to save man. He predetermined the general course and set the boundaries of life on earth. Then He placed man within this format to see what He would do. Those who seek God are led to eternal life and blessing, while those who seek selfish gain and glory are rejected. God does not predestine man's choices, only the general plan and course of life on earth. Does the Bible say this anywhere? It certainly does. Listen close.

Acts 17:24 *God that made the world and all things therein, seeing that he is Lord of heaven and earth, dwelleth not in temples made with hands; 25 Neither is worshipped with men's hands, as though he needed any thing, seeing he giveth to all life, and breath, and all things; 26 And hath **made of one blood all nations of men for to dwell on all the face of the earth, and hath determined the times before appointed, and the bounds of their habitation;** 27 That **they should seek the Lord, if haply they might feel after him, and find him,** though he be not far from every one of us: 28 For in him we live, and move, and have our being; as certain also of your own poets have said, For we are also his offspring. 29 Forasmuch then as we are the offspring of God, we ought not to think that the Godhead is like unto gold, or silver, or stone, graven by art and man's device. 30 And the times of this ignorance God winked at; but **now commandeth all men every where to repent: 31 Because he hath appointed a day, in the which he will judge the world in righteousness by that man whom he hath ordained;** whereof* *he hath given assurance unto all men, in that he hath raised him from the dead.*

You can easily see the part of life that God predestined and controls; and you can also see the part of life that God has left as man's responsibility – man's choices. God's sovereignty is seen in that He is above His creation and will be the ultimate judge and ruler; but God's sovereignty in NO WAY means God controls everything that happens. He is not willing that any should perish, but He plainly leaves this choice in man's realm of responsibility, and waits to see what they will do with it. This makes clear common sense, whereas Calvinistic predestination and sovereignty teaching makes no sense at all. Calvinism when boiled down to its base elements is nothing but predestination of everything, or what they call monergism. Ask any Calvinist who disagrees, "What did God NOT predestinate?" The answer will prove they think God is every player on the field; and every actor on the stage - as though God is just playing chess with himself. NO thinking man can admire, marvel, worship, and appreciate such a God. The Bible never paints this picture of God; but continually we see God holding man accountable for his choices and judging him accordingly.

Sanctification is the rehabilitation training in the clinic. It is the work of the clinic officers along with the Word and the Holy Spirit. We need to be washed with the Word; God's laws need to be written in our hearts and minds; and we thus must be transformed by the renewing of our minds that we might "prove what is that good and acceptable and perfect will of God" (Rom. 12). While justification deals with our crime, sanctification deals with our character. While justification deals with what we have done, sanctification deals with who we are and what

28

we think. We must be cleansed from all the selfishness, pride, rebellion, and ingratitude, or the king can never allow us into his kingdom – it would only endanger his faithful subjects.

The Clinic is the local New Testament church. This is where much of the sanctification and "brain washing" takes place. We need our minds cleansed from the filth of the world and lies of the devil. We need the washing of the water of the word. The ministers of God, who are faithful and true to the Word, will minister to us the Spirit and mind of God as they preach the Word in its purity. God's program for saving us is inseparable from the local assembly of believers called the "church". Anyone who devalues the need and importance to be in and under the training of a local biblical church is still in rebellion to the King. God has given clear teaching on the order, structure, responsibilities, and mission of the local churches. Our book "God's Crucible" deals with these dynamics.

The Badge is the earnest - the seal of God's acceptance and pardon, which is the Holy Spirit's presence and witness in the life of the believer. The Holy Spirit is given as a pledge that we are betrothed to the Lord to be His bride; but this is naturally a probationary time of proving before the actual wedding takes place. The faithful bride has nothing to fear; but she also knows that her blessed position is not unconditionally secure. She knows that unfaithfulness even after being betrothed can cause her to be rejected. The Marriage Supper of The Lamb is the grand event awaiting the faithful (Rev 19). Wearing the badge is the shameless testimony of the believer "in this adulterous and sinful generation". God gives us the earnest of His Spirit as a certainty that He has accepted our repentance, and that we are His children as long as we are faithful and abide in the covenant.

Ro 8:14 *For as many as are **led by the Spirit of God**, **they are the sons of God.** 15 For ye have not received the spirit of bondage again to fear; but ye have received the **Spirit of adoption**, whereby we cry, Abba, Father. 16 The **Spirit itself beareth witness with our spirit, that we are the children of God:** 17 And if children, then heirs; heirs of God, and joint-heirs with Christ; if so be that we suffer with him, that we may be also glorified together.*

Notice our becoming sons and daughters of the king is **not** through being begotten – but through legal adoption. **It is the language of monarchy**: a son or daughter of the King is one of His faithful subjects, and not necessarily a genetic offspring. It is a legal relationship conditioned upon the keeping of a conditional covenant. Consider again:

2Co 6:16 *And what agreement hath the temple of God with idols? for ye are the temple of the living God; as God hath said, I will dwell in them, and walk in them; and I will be their God, and they shall be my people. 17 Wherefore come out from among them, and be ye separate, saith the Lord, and touch not the unclean thing; and I will receive you, 18 **And will be a Father unto you, and ye shall be my sons and daughters, saith the Lord Almighty.** 7:1 **Having** therefore these promises (CONDITIONS), dearly beloved, **let us** cleanse ourselves from all filthiness of the flesh and spirit, perfecting holiness in the fear of God.*

We were children of the devil – how did we change that? We changed our relationship by repenting, coming under God's conditions and receiving His Spirit. We were not begotten by the devil either; but were his children by our adherence to him and being led by his spirit.

Joh 8:44 *Ye are of your father the devil, and the lusts of your father ye will do.*

Eph 2:2 *Wherein in time past ye walked according to the course of this world, according to the prince of the power of the air, **the spirit that now worketh in the children of disobedience:***

In the parable of the tares, it is obvious that being a child of God or of the devil was determined by whose doctrine (seed) you believed, and thus were a product of that seed – either a tare or the wheat. Satan's false gospel produces seeming look-a-likes until the fruit is produced; and then the scandal is discovered, because Satan's doctrine and spirit cannot produce a holy and righteous life.

Mt 13:38 *The field is the world; the good seed are the children of the kingdom; but the tares are the children of the wicked one;*

You are a child of the Lord or of the devil depending on whose doctrine you follow and whose servant you choose to be. Remember that Romans 8:14 said that "as many as are **led** by the Spirit of God, **they** are the **sons** of God." Listen closely again:

Ro 6:16 *Know ye not, that to whom ye yield yourselves servants to obey, his servants ye are to whom ye obey; whether of sin unto death, or of obedience unto righteousness? 17 But God be thanked, that ye were the servants of sin, but ye have obeyed from the heart that form of doctrine which was* *delivered you. 18 Being then made free from sin, ye became the servants of righteousness.*

Jesus was the **only begotten** Son who was therefore of the same substance as the Father. We are sons and daughters adopted through the New Covenant as we repent, believe the gospel, and are led of God's Spirit. This is a conditional covenant relationship as we have clearly seen many times in the verses used. We have the responsibility to maintain this relationship through the means of grace provided in the covenant conditions. Christ living in us is our connection with the Father; and we determine the extent of that reality every day by our attitudes and choices.

Chapter Four

To Work Or Not To Work

In our day there is much confusion concerning salvation. Many think that if we have any part at all to play in our being saved, then we are not trusting Jesus completely. I don't understand why they never consider that obeying carefully what Jesus said is indeed trusting Him completely. If Jesus established the New Covenant, and gave us responsibilities therein, then for us to faithfully fulfill those responsibilities is the essence of trusting Jesus. Those who claim to trust Jesus without doing what He commanded are dangerously presumptuous. **So just what is this "salvation by works" that everyone seems so intent on avoiding?** Is there danger in loving and obeying God too much? Are we in error to strive to "perfect holiness in the fear of God" like Paul exhorted? Are we militating against our Christian liberty to "approve things that are excellent" or "abstain from all appearance of evil" like the apostles told us? Should we wait for God to put us on the narrow way and then push us along to the end?

When the Bible says in *Titus 3:5 "Not by works of righteousness which we have done, but according to his mercy He saved us"* is it declaring that we have nothing to do in our salvation or that working righteousness somehow gets in the way of God's program? Do we not need to

33

repent, believe, confess, or obey?   You would think anyone who passed first grade and had read the New Testament could see the answer; but there are men with much education that are confused on this simple, yet vital point. Think of our parable: was the king's gracious offer and plan due to works of righteousness that the people had done? No, of course not! They were banished for the deeds they had done. They were enemies of the king by wicked works (Col 1:21). The king's decision to offer such a gracious opportunity of reconciliation was certainly not based on any debt he owed these banished people. They had not merited any favor from the king; but actually had merited his disfavor and banishment. The king owed them nothing but condemnation; however this doesn't change the fact that in order for the king to save them, they still must cooperate and follow his program. In order for the king's program to work for their salvation, they had to repent of their enmity, confess their transgressions, comply with the king's demands, cooperate with his program, submit to the laws of his kingdom again, and receive the king as their rightful lord and master.

If I found my enemy had run off the road into the ditch, rolled his car, and was trapped inside, and I stopped to help; would it be because of any debt I owed him, or because he was such a good guy? Not if he was my enemy for no fault of my own. If I stopped to help him out, it would be because of my grace and mercy – not his works or goodness. Now, we know that my help is pure grace, and not due to his works; but do I still expect him to cooperate with my help to get him out? If he will not cooperate and WORK to get out with my help, then I cannot save him, and he will remain trapped in his car. He must do what I say, and cooperate with my salvation,

34

or he will not be saved. If he does obey and cooperate, my decision to save him was still due to my grace and not due to his works.

When we speak of "salvation by works" we are speaking of the **basis** of God's gracious provision, not the **means** needed for us to partake of it. There is a world of difference between the BASIS of God's decision and provision of salvation, and the MEANS necessary for me to partake of his provision. Once my enemy was free and safe, could he boast that he delivered himself? Could he claim that his deliverance was not a gift of grace? No, but he also could tell of his own necessary struggle in cooperation with my deliverance. In the same way Noah could tell of his struggles building the Ark. In the same way Paul says in *2Ti 4:7 "I have fought a good fight, I have finished my course, I have kept the faith: 8 Henceforth there is laid up for me a crown of righteousness, which the Lord, the righteous judge, shall give me at that day: and not to me only, but unto all them also that love his appearing."* Remember it was Paul who said, "not of works lest any man should boast"; and he is not contradicting himself or being inconsistent. This is Gospel Synergism as opposed to Calvinistic Monergism. (See Synergism VS Monergism at www.thefaithoncedelivered.info/web-living_faith_000062.htm)

Say you are starving to death, and I come to save you. I bring a plate of spaghetti and set it before you. I have provided salvation to a starving man by grace, and not due to any debt I owed. Now, will you be saved if you do nothing? No, unless you eat the spaghetti, you will still die. You must partake of the salvation I have provided. Does your partaking of the provision somehow pay for it? No. Does your eating of the spaghetti somehow make my salvation any less of grace? No. Alright, now what would salvation by works be in this scenario? Salvation by works is not you eating of my spaghetti; but salvation by works would be you providing your own spaghetti! See the difference?

According to the Bible "salvation by works" means we atone for our own sins, and thus make ourselves acceptable to God without Jesus' atonement and priesthood. If you have a plan to be saved and accounted righteous before God in the courtroom of heaven without going through God's gracious program that He has provided, then you are seeking to save yourself. However, if you are following God's program and diligently doing all the Savior has commanded, then you are not seeking salvation outside of Christ, but through Christ. Those who claim to be "trusting Jesus only" for salvation, but are not following His program and obeying His commands are just presumptuous fools trusting in their own false concepts. They are actually the ones seeking an alternate route to what God has provided; not the ones striving to live holy and obey Christ.

In our parable, would obedience to the king's commands or obedience to the conditions of the king's covenant be a lack of faith in the king or trusting one's self for salvation? Of course not, it would be the very essence of having faith in the king to diligently follow all his directives. Would obeying the clinic officers and doing what they taught be a lack of faith in the king or seeking to be "saved by my own works"? How foolish to think that following the king's program in any way militates against faith in the king! None of these acts of obedience or submission would make the king's program any less grace – rather it would make the king's grace not in vain! When one refuses to eat God's "spaghetti", His grace in providing for their salvation is in vain. Is it possible for God's grace to be offered or given in vain according to the Scriptures? Yes, we are warned of such. If we do not follow and continue to the end, then the grace provided to save us was in vain. What a shame!

1Co 15:10 *But by the grace of God I am what I am: and his grace which was bestowed upon me* **was not in vain***; but I laboured more abundantly than they all: yet not I, but the grace of God which was with me.*

2Co 6:1 *We then, as workers together with him, beseech you also that ye* **receive not the grace of God in vain***.*

Cooperation with God's salvation program is essential for our final salvation; but that doesn't mean we are saving ourselves or not trusting God to save us. Noah was saved by grace; but he still had to build the ark. Without Noah building the ark in obedience to God, he would not have been saved. Without his compliance with God's commands, he would not have found grace in the eyes of the Lord. Why didn't all the other people find grace in God's eyes and be saved by God's grace? They did not believe God and thus comply with His gracious offer like Noah did. Sure, God could have saved Noah with him doing NOTHING; but that is not how God saves. God is sifting hearts, and His salvation program is designed to weed out those who are not genuine in their faith and repentance.

We've stated that one can be saved by works if they can atone for their own sins or be counted righteous before God's court through their own means. There is another way this can happen. If one of these banished people could prove they had never transgressed the king's commandments at all and thus deserved to be restored without the King's gracious program; then they could show that the king owed them acceptance as a debt and not as grace. In either case "Salvation by works" ceases to be "salvation", and becomes "reward" based on debt, rather than grace. Listen close:

Ro 4:4 *Now to him that worketh is the <u>reward</u> not reckoned of <u>grace</u>, but of <u>debt</u>.*

If one can provide his own spaghetti, then receiving inheritance in God's kingdom is a reward based on debt, not salvation based on grace. If these people thought they could save themselves through their own program by atoning for their own sins and providing their own priesthood that would be acceptable to the king's laws, they would be in the same error as the Jews were in.

Ro 10:1 *Brethren, my heart's desire and prayer to God for Israel is, that they might be saved. 2 For I bear them record that they have a zeal of God, but **not according to knowledge.** 3 For they being ignorant of God's righteousness, and going about to establish their own righteousness, have not submitted themselves unto the righteousness of God. 4 For Christ is the end of the law for righteousness to every one that believeth.*

This is the error the Jews fell into believing that the blood of bulls and goats in their animal sacrifices with their Levitical priesthood was sufficient to give them a righteous standing with God. God's "justification" or "means of obtaining a righteous standing with God" required the atonement of Jesus Christ to do what animal sacrifices could not do. The animal sacrifices and Levitical priesthood were only object lessons to foreshadow Christ's true and sufficient atonement and priesthood.

So, this option of "salvation by my works" is a false hope that got in the way and frustrated God's efforts to save them.

Gal. 2:21 *I do not frustrate the grace of God: for if righteousness* **(Justification)** *come by the law, then Christ is dead in vain.*

Paul knew that the ceremonial laws of animal sacrifice and Levitical priesthood could never give him a righteous standing before God without the atonement of Christ. If it could, then Christ didn't need to die! If one of these banished people could show they had another program as good as the king's that would render them acceptable to the King's court, meet all the King's conditions, and yet not need the King's program, this would be salvation by works – self atonement. To be "saved by works" as the Bible speaks of, either I must have a perfect record of obedience so the Law cannot condemn me, but would only justify me; or I must have a means of self atonement, thereby not needing the atonement and priesthood of Jesus. These are the only two options acknowledged by the Scriptures as "salvation by works" and both are a hopeless dead end of impossibility. **We must eat God's spaghetti or die, we cannot provide our own.**

Chapter Five

Parable of The Great Physician

Once upon a time, there was a race of people who contracted a disease. This disease was a disease of the heart and mind that led men to live as fools. As the disease progressed, they became extremely selfish, wicked, proud, and their appetites became base and animalistic. There was a great physician who alone could properly treat and cure this disease. Out of compassion, he offered his services free of charge, for he knew they could not otherwise afford them. Being that it was a fatal disease if left unchecked, and was very complex; it was of the utmost importance that those who applied to the doctor for help put their complete faith in His protocol and did exactly as He said. There was a strict change of diet; there were exercises that had to be performed regularly; and there were exercises not only for the body, but also for the mind and heart. They had to read and meditate on stories and instructional materials from a special book; and they had to even memorize portions of this book. All of this, along with the special injections regularly administered by the physician would lead to renewed life and health.

The disease had led them to exercise their heart with covetous practices, but now they had to exercise themselves rather unto godliness. They had to be transformed by the renewing of their minds through the stories and teaching of the physician. They had to meet regularly in support groups and rehearse the stories and teachings of the physician or they would begin to slip back into their old appetites and the disease would again make progress. The diseased appetite was for that which was forbidden and animalistic; but the healthy appetite was for that which was righteous and Spiritual. The new life of wellness was completely dependent upon their faith in the physician and thus continuing in His wellness program – taking the medicine, reading the stories, following the diet, and doing their daily exercises – in this way alone could they overcome their disease and walk at liberty from it. If they continued to overcome, they were able to live free of the disease; but as soon as they slacked their faithfulness or compromised the program, the disease would again start showing symptoms.

It was an enemy of these people who had developed the disease and helped them contract it. He hoped to eradicate their entire race. In order to defeat the Great Physician's efforts, he endeavored to break down the patient's faith in the doctor's orders. The doctor strictly forbade them to yield their members as instruments of unrighteousness; but this enemy set up false clinics that taught them to have faith in their own judgment and touted the motto, "Yield Responsibly". He insisted they could yield according to convenience and what they deemed expedient. Other clinics tried to convince the people that they could not keep from yielding to their diseased hearts, but that this would not affect their final wellness. The doctor knew, however, that every small surrender to the disease only broke down their resistance, and rendered them less able to resist it in the future. Every surrender to their depravity also damaged the person's discernment and ability to recognize their need and danger. If the people didn't do what the Great Physician told them, he would not administer the crucial injections of his special medicine. Thus the battle for men's lives also became a battle between faith in the doctor and faith in one's own judgment.

The physician's services were completely free. The treatment was so expensive no one could have afforded it, so He didn't charge anyone for it — it was a free gift. The more interaction they had with the doctor and the more they were faithful to follow the program, the more they benefited and experienced wellness. So...

Did their obedience to the doctor and faithfulness to the program diminish their indebtedness to the physician or increase it? Increase it of course! Go to your doctor more often and see if your bill goes up or down. People today are saying that our striving to obey the Lord Jesus is somehow trying to pay for our salvation; but in reality it makes us more indebted to the Great Physician of our souls. YES, obedience to the doctor DOES affect whether we will be saved; but it in NO WAY diminished the grace of the doctor or our indebtedness to him.

Would anyone in their right mind think that following the protocol or obeying the doctor was somehow trying to pay for his services? Would anyone in their right mind think that faithfulness and diligence in obeying the doctor would somehow frustrate the grace of the doctor because he would think they were trying to pay for his services??

This kind of insanity doesn't happen in real life, but only in theology books.

Would anyone think that the doctor was opposed to their faithful diligence in following His protocol, because he wanted all the glory for healing them; and with them doing what he said, they would get part of the glory??? Only a Calvinist could come up with something like that. If I do all that Jesus says, then in reality I am giving Him more glory. The more faith I place in the doctor, the more glory and honor I give him. To say that I am taking glory to myself because I claim that the **choice** to trust the doctor is due to my free-will, is monergistic nonsense. If I told you I have 100% faith in my doctor, and I do everything the man says; am I then getting glory to myself or giving it to him? If you can see this in real life, then you should see it in theology as well.

Can you imagine one patient saying to another — "Do you think that all your diligent obedience to the doctor is going to make you well more than I?" or "Do you think because you obey the doctor more faithfully you are a better patient and will experience more wellness?" or "Why are you so concerned about "obedience", don't you know that the doctor's services are free and not based on your obedience?? Don't you know that we are all just 'sickies', saved by the doctor's grace — why do you think that obeying the doctor makes you any more saved than the rest of us who just believe in the doctor, but don't obey him?" Only an antinomian could dream up such silliness. You may think I am exaggerating; but I'm not. I've heard such statements many times concerning salvation through Christ. I was raised in the false teachings and went to their colleges.

The Physician promised them life through His program; but what if they don't continue in it? Does that lessen the validity of the promise? Could they expect to have the life promised when they didn't faithfully follow the program? Could they claim to believe in this doctor, if they didn't completely and thoroughly follow the program to the end? **Every degree of variance from the program would be a degree of unbelief in the doctor. The doctor only promised their healing if they put their complete faith in him.**

As with the doctor's program, the salvation that Jesus offers is a program for our healing and restoration to spiritual health. Life and wellness comes at the end of the "narrow way", not at the beginning. Jesus clearly said, *"Strait is the gate, and narrow is the way that <u>leadeth unto life</u>..."* The apostle Paul in Romans 6 is very clear on this matter as he states in verse 22, *"But now being made free from sin, and become servants to God, ye have your fruit unto holiness, and the <u>end</u> everlasting life.*
Peter says in 1 Peter 1:9, *"...Receiving the <u>end</u> of your faith, even the salvation of your souls".*

Did Jesus or the apostles promise a "gos-pill" that would cure you by just taking one? Or did Jesus imply that your salvation was a process where you had a part to play and the final result came at the end of the program? Any honest perusal of Scripture would clearly answer that question.

***Mt 7:21** Not every one that saith unto me, Lord, Lord, shall enter into the kingdom of heaven; **but he that doeth the will of my Father which is in heaven**. 22 Many will say to me in that day, Lord, Lord, have we not prophesied in thy name? and in thy* name have cast out devils? and in thy name done many wonderful works? 23 And then will I profess unto them, I never knew you: depart from me, ye that work iniquity. 24 **Therefore whosoever heareth these sayings of mine, and doeth them, I will liken him unto a wise man, which built his house upon a rock:** 25 And the rain descended, and the floods came, and the winds blew, and beat upon that house; and it fell not: for it was founded upon a rock. 26 **And every one that heareth these sayings of mine, and doeth them not, shall be likened unto a foolish man, which built his house upon the sand:** 27 And the rain descended, and the floods came, and the winds blew, and beat upon that house; and it fell: and great was the fall of it. 28 And it came to pass, when Jesus had ended these sayings, the people were astonished at his doctrine: 29 For he taught them as one having authority, and not as the scribes.

Joh 8:31 Then said Jesus to those Jews which believed on him, If ye **continue in my word**, then are ye my disciples indeed; 32 And ye shall know the truth, and the truth shall make you free....51 Verily, verily, I say unto you, If a man **keep my saying**, he shall never see death.

Ro 6:16 Know ye not, that to whom ye yield yourselves servants to obey, his servants ye are to whom ye obey; whether of sin unto death, or of obedience unto righteousness? 17 But God be thanked, that ye were the servants of sin, but **ye have obeyed from the heart that form of doctrine which was delivered you.** 18 Being then made free from sin, ye became the servants of righteousness. 19 I speak after the manner of men because of the infirmity of your flesh: for as ye have yielded your members servants to uncleanness and to iniquity unto iniquity; even **so now yield your members servants to righteousness unto holiness.** 20 For when ye were the servants of sin, ye were free from righteousness. 21 What fruit had ye then in those things whereof ye are now ashamed? for the end of those things is death. 22 But now being made free from sin, *and become servants to God, **ye have your fruit unto holiness, and the <u>end</u> everlasting life.***

1Ti 4:16 *Take heed unto thyself, and unto the doctrine;* **continue in them: for in doing this thou shalt both save thyself, and them that hear thee.**

He 5:8 *Though he were a Son, yet learned he obedience by the things which he suffered; 9 And being made perfect, he became the author of eternal salvation **unto all them that <u>obey</u> him;** 10 Called of God an high priest after the order of Melchisedec.*

Yes, forgiveness comes in a moment of time when a man repents and God accepts his repentance; however ultimate salvation is at the end of one's race of faith (He 12) – the **end** of the narrow way that **leadeth** to life. Our justification must be maintained through our High Priest, and is not a "done deal". Remember the man in the parable of Christ who had his forgiveness revoked? This is a sobering possibility.

Chapter Six

What Laws Govern Grace?

Everything God does or says is based on eternal laws and principles of righteousness. God's righteousness is the "Art of Appropriateness". God's divine wisdom is seen in His perfect appropriateness. The Law of God and His dealings with man are for us a study in appropriateness. God's grace, mercy, love, justice, and judgment can all be summed up as the "most appropriate thing to do under the circumstances". God is unchanging in His moral judgments, and when the same circumstances exist, He will always give the same judgment call; because God cannot improve on Himself. I cannot emphasize this principle enough; as it is the cure of almost every heresy I know. God's goal is to bring man into line with His appropriateness in every area:

Ro 8:3 *For what the law could not do, in that it was weak through the flesh, God sending his own Son in the likeness of sinful flesh, and for sin, condemned sin in the flesh: 4 **That the righteousness of the law might be fulfilled in us**, who walk not after the flesh, but after the Spirit.*

This "righteousness of the Law" being fulfilled in us is the appropriateness of God's Laws being lived out in our lives. God's grace ALWAYS operates in this same realm of appropriateness. God cannot and will not exercise grace inappropriately. When men understand this, many false concepts of salvation will vanish.

Do you realize that where there is no law, demand, or plumb-line, there can be no grace? If you have no deadline on your payment, then you cannot have a "grace period". However, a "grace period" does not deliver you from your obligations altogether; but simply helps you remedy your failure. Grace can be applied inappropriately and when this happens, it ceases to be grace, and becomes lasciviousness – the absence of appropriateness (Jude 3). When grace is extended as more than helping the fallen to get back up and do their duty, it becomes damaging to those who receive it, and all others involved.

If a dangerous murderer is released back into society because the judge wanted to be "gracious", we immediately see this as inappropriate. This grace is a crime against society, and not a noble move on the judge's part. There are laws that govern and determine when grace is appropriate, and when it becomes lawlessness - the destruction of law and order. Wolves only desire the shepherd to be gracious so they can get another chance to kill a lamb. When the shepherd is gracious to a dangerous wolf, is he being gracious to his flock or his wife and children? Jude warned of men who were "turning the grace of our God into lasciviousness". In doing this they automatically were denying the Lordship of God and Christ. Grace inappropriately given tears down law, order, authority, and the safety of the faithful.

If you are forgiven your debt by the grace of the storekeeper, then it only means you should have been paying for the groceries, and not that the storekeeper's prices were the problem. If your debt was forgiven by the storekeeper's grace, it doesn't mean all the goods are free from now on, or that storekeepers should not charge for their merchandise; but the continued obligation to pay for the groceries still exists. Jesus washed your record clean by grace; but the obligation to obey God is still there, and God's grace cannot remove that; but can only provide a means to help you get back up and do your duty. Jesus as our high priest fills that gap between our obligation and our lack of meeting it; **but only while we are striving to meet it (I Jn 1:7)**. As we repent of our crookedness and strive to line up with God's plumb-line, Jesus acts as our High Priest and thus graciously applies his atonement to us to keep our record clean before God (He 7:25). God's grace provides a remedy, but doesn't do away with our obligation to line up with God's law or plumb-line.

God's grace demands repentance and striving; but makes a way for your lack of perfection while doing so. Grace never surrenders or condemns or compromises the law (See Chap. 10). In fact, God's grace is for the very purpose of bringing us into line with His holy law (Ro 8:3-4). Grace works on a principle that demands my heart and intentions be genuine; but has mercy on my ignorance and weakness in actually performing perfectly. I must be genuine in my repentance and desire to please God; but God accepts this exercise of faith and counts it to me for righteousness by grace; because my sanctification is a process and my perfection in performance is not complete yet. This principle is clearly stated in 2 Cor. 8:12:

2Co 8:12 *For if there be **first a willing mind,** it is **accepted according to that a man hath,** and **not according to that he hath not.***

2 Cor. 8:12 gives us the very principle upon which our salvation rests. Paul is speaking in the context of us pleasing God with monetary offerings, but it is the same principle for us pleasing God in any area. Pleasing God means "finding grace or favor in the sight of the Lord" like Noah did.

Gen 6:8 *But Noah found grace in the eyes of the LORD.*

Noah was saved by God's grace just like we are; and he became eligible for this grace by:

- First having a willing mind and heart to please God;
- Second, giving God all that was in his power to give.

God accepted this by grace, which opened the door for God to pardon Noah and wash him in the blood of Jesus. In God's government it is not even legal to offer grace to one who has transgressed God's holy law without an atonement being made (See ch. 10). God's grace sets aside the penalty of the law, due to the atonement, while I am being rehabilitated. In this way God can be JUST while also being the JUSTIFIER of those who believe in Jesus.

Heb 11:7 *By faith Noah, being warned of God of things not seen as yet, **moved with fear, prepared an ark** to the **saving of his house;** by the which he condemned the world, and **became heir of the righteousness (justification) which is by faith.***

52

The word "righteousness" in the New Testament often means "justification", i.e. obtaining a righteous record or standing before God. God's gracious justification through the cleansing of Christ's blood, which gives us a righteous record and standing before God, is only given to those who <u>walk</u> by faith, and thus are faithful (Heb. 5:9; 11:6). God seeing my genuine faith is the key that allows Him to justly wash my record with the blood of His Son; and thus give me a righteous standing before Him. Without my exercise of faith in Christ, it would not be right to apply His atonement to my case. Abraham's faith is seen in giving to God what he could give with a willing mind/heart. In this he became the father of the faithful (Gal. 3:9).

Gen 26:5...Abraham obeyed my voice, and kept my charge, my commandments, my statutes, and my laws.

God had commanded him, "Walk before me and be thou perfect" (Gen. 17:1). Was God asking something that Abraham could not give? Jesus commands the same thing of us:

Mt 5:48 Be ye therefore **perfect**, even as your Father which is in heaven is perfect.

Is Jesus commanding more than we can perform? No, He is not. He is not commanding us to offer perfect performance or a perfect record of obedience; because He knows this is impossible until we are rehabilitated/sanctified completely. He is commanding us to have a sincere heart desire and whole hearted effort to please God with the light and ability we have. It is the same principle as:

53

Mt 22:37 *"Thou shalt love the Lord thy God with **all thy** heart, and with **all thy** soul, and with **all thy** mind."*

I'm not asked to love God with all **your** heart; all **Paul's** heart; or all **Jesus'** heart; but with all **MY** heart. This I can give if I truly surrender and strive to do so – this is what the Bible says is having a "perfect" heart before God. This is not "sinless perfectionism" or "salvation by works", as neither of those positions require Christ's atonement for salvation. Being "perfect" in the Biblical sense is what God requires before He will pardon us and wash us with Christ's atoning blood. It means **genuineness** in my repentance and faith. Sometimes it also means "mature" or "complete" depending on the context. Do a word study on the word "perfect" in the Bible.

We can take the principle of 2 Cor. 8:12 and state it in many different, yet synonymous ways:

1. *For if there be first a willing mind, it is accepted according to that a man hath, and not according to that he hath not.*
2. *If there first be the obedience of faith, which we can offer, it is accepted in the place of perfect obedience, which we cannot offer.*
3. *God's grace is seen in accepting what we can give – the obedience of faith/willing mind; and not requiring what we cannot give – a perfect record of obedience. His acceptance makes us eligible for the atonement and priesthood of Christ to cleanse us and keep us clean.*

In 2 Cor. 8:12 the word translated "willing mind" is prothumia, (proth-oo-mee'-ah), predisposition, i.e. alacrity; which means cheerful readiness or cheerful willingness. You can see this in the following verses:

54

Ac 17:11 *These were more noble than those in Thessalonica, in that they received the word with all **readiness of mind**, and searched the scriptures daily, whether those things were so.*

2 Co 8:11 *Now therefore perform the doing of it; that as there was a **readiness to will**, so there may be a performance also out of that which ye have. **12** For if there be first a **willing mind**, it is accepted according to that a man hath, and not according to that he hath not.*

This is the same principle which we see in the next two verses:

2 Co 9:7 *Every man according as he purposeth in his heart, so let him give; not grudgingly, or of necessity: **for God loveth a cheerful giver.***

Ac 11:29 *Then the disciples, **every man according to his ability, determined** to send relief unto the brethren which dwelt in Judaea:*

God sees this as righteous – "they cheerfully determined to do their best!" This is the Spirit of Psalms 119:

1 Blessed are the undefiled in the way, who walk in the law of the LORD.
*2 Blessed are they that keep his testimonies, and **that seek him with the whole heart.***
3 They also do no iniquity: they walk in his ways.
4 Thou hast commanded us to keep thy precepts diligently.
*5 **O that my ways were directed to keep thy statutes!***
6 Then shall I not be ashamed, when I have respect unto all thy commandments.
7 I will praise thee with uprightness of heart, when I shall have learned thy righteous judgments.
*...32 I will **run** the way of thy commandments, when thou shalt enlarge my heart.*

This is what God is looking for, so He can righteously pour out His grace and mercy. This is all He requires from man, because He knows we have fallen, and cannot atone for our own sins.

Micah 6:6 *Wherewith shall I come before the LORD, and bow myself before the high God? shall I come before him with burnt offerings, with calves of a year old?*
7 Will the LORD be pleased with thousands of rams, or with ten thousands of rivers of oil? shall I give my firstborn for my transgression, the fruit of my body for the sin of my soul?

This man sees the futility of trying to atone for his own sins. What is the answer?

Micah 6:8 *He hath shewed thee, O man, what is good; and* **what doth the LORD require of thee, but to do justly, and to love mercy, and to walk humbly with thy God?**

We cannot save ourselves; but we can offer a cheerful submission and obedience to the best of our ability. God accepts this living obeying faith according to what we have to offer; and not according to what we do not have to offer! God knows when we are doing our best.

Deut 5:29 *O that there were* **such an heart in them**, *that they would* **fear me**, *and* **keep all my commandments always**, *that it might be well with them, and with their children for ever!*

Heb 8:10 *For this is the covenant that I will make with the house of Israel after those days, saith the Lord;* **I will put my laws into their mind, and write them in their hearts:** *and I will be to them a God, and* **they shall be to me a people***:*

Giving ourselves to God cheerfully is our reasonable service:

Rom. 12:1 I beseech you therefore, brethren, by the mercies of God, that ye present your bodies a living sacrifice, holy, acceptable unto God, **which is your reasonable service**.

Titus 2:11 For the **grace of God that bringeth salvation** hath appeared to all men,
12 **Teaching us that, denying ungodliness and worldly lusts, we should live soberly, righteously, and godly, in this present world;**
13 Looking for that blessed hope, and the glorious appearing of the great God and our Saviour Jesus Christ;
14 Who gave himself for us, **that he might redeem us from all iniquity, and purify unto himself a peculiar people, zealous of good works.**

From Genesis to Revelation God's plan of salvation by grace has been the same in principle; and those who knew God's ways also understood what He expected if they were to find grace in His sight.

1Ch 28:9 And thou, Solomon my son, know thou the God of thy father, and **serve** him with a **perfect heart** and with a **willing mind:** for the LORD searcheth all hearts, and understandeth all the imaginations of the thoughts: if thou **seek** him, **he will be found of thee;** but if thou forsake him, he will cast thee off for ever.

The willing mind is not accepted alone, but is accepted along with us doing what we can do, and giving what we can give. This is the only righteous way God can accept us and wash us in the blood of Jesus, and make us His children.

2 Cor. 6:17 Wherefore come out from among them, and be ye separate, saith the Lord, and touch not the unclean thing; **and I will receive you,**

*18 And **will be a Father unto you**, and **ye shall be my sons and daughters**, saith the Lord Almighty*

I could fill volumes with illustrations of this principle from Scripture; but I'm trying not to over burden you. Bear with me now as I explain a very important chapter dealing with this very subject. Please pay close attention.

Rom 10:1 *Brethren, my heart's desire and prayer to God for Israel is, that they might be saved.*
2 For I bear them record that they have a zeal of God, but not according to knowledge.
3 For they being ignorant of God's righteousness **(justification)***, and going about to establish their own righteousness* **(justification)***, have not submitted themselves unto the righteousness of God* **(God's way of justifying men).**
4 For Christ is the end **(goal and aim)** *of the law for righteousness* **(justification)** *to every one that believeth.*
5 For Moses describeth the righteousness **(justification)** *which is of the law* **(alone without grace)***, That the man which doeth those things shall live by them.* **(perfect obedience = life)**
6 But the righteousness **(justification)** *which is of faith speaketh on this wise, Say not in thine heart, Who shall ascend into heaven? (that is, to bring Christ down from above:)*
7 Or, Who shall descend into the deep? (that is, to bring up Christ again from the dead.)

Paul is adapting a passage from the Old Testament to illustrate the difference between justification by God's plumb-line alone, which demands perfect obedience; and justification by grace, which demands us doing what we can do – and that being accepted by grace. The passage Paul is adapting is Deut. 30:10-16

Deut 30:10 *If thou shalt hearken unto the voice of the LORD thy God, to keep his commandments and his statutes which are* *written in this book of the law, and **if thou turn unto the LORD thy God with all thine heart, and with all thy soul***.

11 ¶ For this commandment which I command thee this day, it is not hidden from thee, neither is it far off.

12 It is not in heaven, that thou shouldest say, Who shall go up for us to heaven, and bring it unto us, that we may hear it, and do it?

13 Neither is it beyond the sea, that thou shouldest say, Who shall go over the sea for us, and bring it unto us, that we may hear it, and do it?

14 But the word is very nigh unto thee, in thy mouth, and in thy heart, that thou mayest do it.

15 ¶ See, I have set before thee this day life and good, and death and evil;

16 In that I command thee this day to love the LORD thy God, to walk in his ways, and to keep his commandments and his statutes and his judgments, that thou mayest live and multiply: and the LORD thy God shall bless thee in the land whither thou goest to possess it.

What is the point? This passage in Deuteronomy is dealing with God's people getting right **after** they have been carried away into captivity due to sin. What if they want to turn their hearts back to God and obey all his Laws, but they don't have a complete copy, and can't obtain it?

"Who shall go over the sea for us, and bring it unto us, that we may hear it, and do it?"

Are they lost without hope? NO! Praise the Lord! God never expected perfect obedience, but a **perfect heart** – a sincere desire and effort to obey what they **did have**. This was "nigh" them, and they could do it anywhere. Paul uses this to illustrate the difference between justification before God through Law alone without grace; and then justification through God's gracious acceptance of me doing that which I can and know to do. In Romans he adapts the passage to someone in the New Covenant thinking they must be perfect and know all Christ's will:

10:6 But the righteousness **(justification)** *which is of faith speaketh on this wise, <u>Say not in thine heart, Who shall ascend into heaven? (that is, to bring Christ down from above:)</u>*
7 Or<u>, Who shall descend into the deep? (that is, to bring up Christ again from the dead.)</u>
8 But what saith it? <u>The word is nigh thee</u>, even in thy mouth, and in thy heart: that is, the word of faith, which we preach;
9 That if thou shalt confess with thy mouth the Lord Jesus, and shalt believe in thine heart that God hath raised him from the dead, thou shalt be saved.

Since Christ is the culmination and climax of the Law concerning our justification; Paul replaces Moses' Law in the passage with Christ's will and teaching – it is the same principle (Jesus is the Word). If you confess Jesus as your Lord and sincerely believe with your heart, you don't have to perfectly "know" it all, or perfectly "do" it all. Paul is showing that the principle of justification through a living, striving faith is taught in the Old Testament; and is God's only means of saving sinners in the New Testament as well as the Old Testament. The Jews went about to establish self atonement/justification through keeping Moses' Law apart from Christ, and thought God owed them justification (declaration of righteousness) as a debt. They vainly assumed the blood of bulls and goats could take away sins apart from Christ's sacrifice and the grace of God. Paul continues:

10:10 For with the heart man believeth unto righteousness; and with the mouth confession is made unto salvation.

60

*11 For **the scripture saith,** "Whosoever believeth on him shall not be ashamed."*

*12 ¶ For there is no difference between the Jew and the Greek: for the same Lord over all is **rich unto all that call upon him.***

13 For "whosoever shall call upon the name of the Lord shall be saved."

Notice Paul is quoting the Old Testament in order to establish his doctrine. "Believing unto justification" and "confessing unto salvation" are the same as "calling upon the name of the Lord". This term refers to the sincere worship and service of the true God in the OT and NT – look it up. This speaks of a living obeying faith unto the end of ones' life (I Pet. 1:9; Rom. 16:26). This shows that salvation by grace is God's gracious acceptance of what we can give; which makes it right for Him then to apply the atonement to us and wash us clean. As long as we abide in this faith "walking in the Light", we are safe and will be saved when we finish our course.

Maybe this principle can be understood better if we put it into the realm of the home. If a child has done their best, but has nevertheless failed; and the parent is cross and merciless; we charge them with not being gracious. If the child did their best and failed; and the parent draws them close in loving forgiving acceptance; then we say the parent is gracious and merciful. If the child is rebellious, deceitful, self-justifying, lazy, and sneaky; yet the parent draws them close in loving forgiving acceptance; we don't call the parent "gracious" but foolish and guilty of producing a monster! The grace becomes lasciviousness when the child is not striving to please. Grace is only virtuous and noble when given to one who has repented, confessed, made restitution where possible, and is now striving to be righteous. Grace given when it is not appropriate is a lack of wise government; but grace given appropriately is part of being a wise leader. God's grace is always given appropriately, and never so as to damage righteousness or weaken holiness.

Here is the principle again in the Parable of the Talents:

Mt 25:15 *And unto one he gave five talents, to another two, and to another one; to every man **according to his several ability**; and straightway took his journey.*

What happened to the man who did not do what he could do with what his lord had given him? Did the lazy, unfaithful servant receive grace?

Mt 25:30 *And cast ye the unprofitable servant into outer darkness: there shall be weeping and gnashing of teeth.*

The true grace of God is consistent with demanding obedience to God's Holy Law. Offering grace without demanding us to obey according to our ability is "turning the grace of God into lasciviousness" i.e. turning grace into lawlessness or "looseness" on God's part.

Jude 3 *Beloved, when I gave all diligence to write unto you of the common salvation, it was needful for me to write unto you, and exhort you that ye **should earnestly contend for the faith which was once delivered unto the saints.***
*4 For there are certain men crept in unawares, who were before of old ordained to this condemnation, ungodly men, **turning the grace of our God into lasciviousness**, and denying the only Lord God, and our Lord Jesus Christ.*

"Denying the Lord" means denying his "lordship" or denying that you have to obey him! This makes God's grace in reality a capitulation to sin; destruction of His

Law; and confusion concerning what salvation is all about -- but this is what is being preached in our day! It is amazing that the attack on God's Grace began while the apostles were still alive! All the apostles had to combat Satan's presentations of "false grace". Read Peter's first epistle and you will find him presenting "true grace".

1Pe 1:9 *Receiving the **end of your faith**, even the salvation of your souls...*

*13 Wherefore gird up the loins of your mind, be sober, and **hope to the end** for the grace that is to be brought unto you at the revelation of Jesus Christ;*

*14 **As obedient children**, not fashioning yourselves according to the former lusts in your ignorance:*

*15 But as he which hath called you is holy, **so be ye holy in all manner of conversation;***

16 Because it is written (OT), *Be ye holy; for I am holy.*

*17 and if ye **call on the Father...*** (Remember this term? - Rom 10:13)

*...who without respect of persons judgeth according to every man's work, **pass the time of your sojourning here in fear:***

18 Forasmuch as ye know that ye were not redeemed with corruptible things, as silver and gold, from your vain conversation received by tradition from your fathers;

19 But with the precious blood of Christ, as of a lamb without blemish and without spot:..

4:17 *For the time is come that judgment must begin at the house of God: and if it first begin at us, what shall the end be of them that obey not the gospel of God?*

*18 And if the **righteous scarcely be saved**, where shall the ungodly and the sinner appear?*

*19 Wherefore let them that suffer according to the will of God **commit the keeping of their souls to him <u>in well doing,</u>** as unto a faithful Creator...*

5:12 ...I have written briefly, exhorting, and testifying that this is the **true grace of God** wherein ye stand.

Chapter Seven

How Does Faith Work?

William Tyndale was a brave and sincere man who determined to translate the Bible into the English language while, according to the state church, it was still illegal to do so. His translation was a wonderful work of God's providence, and was used extensively in the later King James' Version and other English versions. I personally think his translation of Hebrews 11:1 is more accurate in sense and meaning.

Heb 11:1 (Tyndale) *Faith is a sure confidence of things which are hoped for, and a certainty of things which are not seen.*

One who has a hope set before him; puts his confidence in that hope; and then acts upon that confidence, is exercising **faith**. Faith must be placed in a true and valid hope or it is mere presumption and fantasy. If you were in the desert and saw a large body of water to save you from your thirst, would you have a valid hope to place your faith in? Well, if it were a mirage, then your faith would be placed in an illegitimate hope, and thus would be a great disappointment. If it were truly an oasis, your faith would be in a legitimate hope, and your faith would cause you to run and drink and rejoice. If you just stood still in unbelief, then you did not exercise faith in this hope set before you. Faith is acting upon a hope. Faith is doing what is necessary to embrace and obtain the hope set before us.

Heb 11:6 *But without faith it is impossible to please him: for he that cometh to God must believe that he is,* **and** *that he is a rewarder of them that diligently seek him.*

The Bible says very plainly that faith without the corresponding works is dead. To claim to put your faith in a proper hope, but to then not act upon that faith is simply a lie. Faith without works is dead. Dead faith does not save the soul, nor obtain the hope. **If** God promised that "if you just did NOTHING", He would come and save you and take you to Heaven, then exercising faith in that promise would be to do NOTHING; **but God never made any such promise**. All God's promises give us something to **do**, and therefore faith in God demands we are doing something to meet the conditions of the promises and commands.

If my son, Micah, and I were on a wilderness trek with an experienced guide; and we were suddenly confronted by a large bear. The guide turns to Micah and says, "Son, you stay calm and do exactly what I tell you." Now, I look at Micah and say, "Son, **believe** in the guide"; or "Son, **trust** the guide"; or "Son, **follow** what he says"; or "Son, **hold fast your confidence in the guide to the end**"; or "Son, **receive** this man as your guide" or "Son, **have faith** in the guide" -- **I have said the same thing!** Wouldn't it be foolish for Micah to look at me and say, "Dad, does 'trust the guide' mean I have to obey him?"

Jesus is our Shepherd, Guide, Lord, Master, Savior, Captain, etc. He says, "Follow me"; "Trust me"; "Keep my word"; "believe in me"; etc. etc. etc. How on earth can anyone not see that faith in Him requires obedience to Him?! Anyone who reads the Bible with an unbiased mind can see this. The apostles knew that to be saved they must obey "the faith" Jesus taught. Jesus taught them the truth of the gospel, which is called "the faith of Christ" (the faith Christ taught); and this faith demands its adherents pursue a certain course of life. If we have faith in Christ, then we obey the faith or doctrine He taught.

Rom 1:5 *By whom we have received grace and apostleship, for* **obedience to the faith** *among all nations, for his name:*

Now listen to what they hoped to accomplish by spreading the faith of Christ among all nations:

Rom 16:25 *Now to him that is of power to stablish you according to my gospel, and the preaching of Jesus Christ, according to the revelation of the mystery, which was kept secret since the world began, 26 But now is made manifest, and by the scriptures of the prophets, according to the commandment of the everlasting God,* **made known to all nations for** <u>the obedience of faith</u>:

By obeying and propagating the faith of Christ among all nations they would produce obedience to Christ based on faith in Him, His teachings, and His promises. The obedience of faith is the true value of faith; because faith without this obedience is dead and worthless to God.

As we've stated earlier, if I were a physician, and I wanted to treat and heal your disease, what would the most important issue be? You must have enough faith in me to obey me! You might believe I am a doctor; but faith in me could only be real if you did what I said. Faith without works would be dead, and you would be dead too, because I couldn't help you unless you obeyed and did what I said. Jesus cannot help you unless you put your faith in Him to the point that you obey and follow his protocol. Don't say you have faith in Jesus, unless you are taking His prescription fully and not altering it to your own liking. If you change the prescription at all it only means you have more faith in yourself than your doctor!

Many have said that Paul and James were not in harmony concerning their ideas about faith and works. This idea comes from the Devil's clinics. They were both inspired of the same God, and both taught the same gospel. So, how do we reconcile the following passages of Scripture concerning faith and works?

{James writing}
Ja 2:14 *¶ What doth it profit, my brethren, though a man say he hath faith, and have not works? can faith save him?*
15 If a brother or sister be naked, and destitute of daily food,
16 And one of you say unto them, Depart in peace, be ye warmed and filled; notwithstanding ye give them not those things which are needful to the body; what doth it profit?
17 Even so faith, if it hath not works, is dead, being alone.
18 Yea, a man may say, Thou hast faith, and I have works: shew me thy faith without thy works, and I will shew thee my faith by my works.
19 Thou believest that there is one God; thou doest well: the devils also believe, and tremble.
20 But wilt thou know, O vain man, that faith without works is dead?
*21 Was not Abraham our father **justified by works**, when he had offered Isaac his son upon the altar?*

68

22 Seest thou how faith wrought with his works, and by works was faith made perfect?

23 And the scripture was fulfilled which saith, Abraham believed God, and it was imputed unto him for righteousness: and he was called the Friend of God.

*24 **Ye see then how that by works a man is justified, and not by faith only.***

*25 Likewise also was not Rahab the harlot **justified by works**, when she had received the messengers, and had sent them out another way?*

*26 For as the body without the spirit is dead, so **faith without works is dead** also.*

{Paul writing}

Eph 2:8 *For by grace are ye saved **through faith**; and that not of yourselves: it is the gift of God: 9 **Not of works**, lest any man should boast.*

Ro 3:20 *Therefore by the deeds of the law there shall no flesh be justified in his sight: for by the law is the knowledge of sin.*

James says faith without works is dead, and that we are justified by works and faith together. Paul says we are saved by faith and not works. What is the answer? The answer is very simple and related to our parables.

First, the apostles are speaking of two different concepts when they are using the term "works". James is speaking of faith in action, like us obeying the doctor and taking his medicine because we have faith in him. These works are necessary or our faith is dead as we have already spoken of. Paul is speaking about works of perfect performance or works to atone for our own sins, so that our righteous standing with God is a reward based on a debt God owes us, rather than grace to the undeserving (Ro 4). Paul in Ephesians and Romans is saying, "You cannot save yourself, and must put faith in God's gracious program"; while James is saying, "You'd better exercise your faith, not just sit on it".   When Paul speaks of "works" or "deeds of the Law", he is speaking of men striving to save themselves with their own methods.   When James speaks of "works", he is speaking of men actually following God's method, not just talking about it. Paul was saying, "You cannot provide your own spaghetti"; while James was saying, "You must eat the spaghetti God has set before you".

If we can heal ourselves, then we need no doctor, and we are "saved by our works" and not grace. However, if we are sick and cannot save ourselves, we must put faith in the doctor and do all he says, thus being saved by a faith that works. One "works" is speaking of me saving myself without the doctor; while the other "works" is speaking of me putting faith in the doctor and doing all he says. There is a world of difference in the two concepts called "works"; and Paul and James agree 100% on what they are saying. They are simply correcting two opposite ditches that people fall into. One group thinks they don't need the doctor/savior; and the other group thinks they don't have to obey the doctor/savior. If we would listen to both apostles as God inspired men, then we would stay out of both ditches, and find the middle of the road, i.e. "We must put our faith in the doctor and do all he says, because we cannot save ourselves with our own remedy."

Noah had to act upon his faith and build the ark, but the Bible says Noah was saved by finding grace in the eyes of the Lord. Noah was saved by a gracious program God devised; but that program required him to work hard on an ark. Without grace Noah would have been destroyed with everyone else, because Noah was a fallen man who could not save himself or atone for his own sins. Jesus had to die for Noah's sins as much as mine, but because Noah believed God, walked with Him, and obeyed Him, He found grace in God's eyes, and received the plan for the ark. He followed the plan and saved his house.

Heb 11:6 But without faith it is impossible to please him: for he that cometh to God must believe that he is, and that he is a rewarder of them that diligently seek him.
7 By **faith** Noah, being warned of God of things not seen as yet, **moved** with **fear**, **prepared an ark** to the **saving of his house**; by the which he condemned the world, and **became heir of the righteousness which is by faith.**

Are you paying close attention to the words? Noah saved his house by moving with fear and preparing an Ark; but this was not salvation by works – **Paul, not James,** clearly says this was **salvation by FAITH**. He became heir of the righteousness of faith i.e. the "righteous standing with God" called "justification" which Paul says is by FAITH. **He was justified by faith and works together, just like James says!** This seems so logical and understandable! Why all the confusion? I'll tell you why. It is a part of Satan's plan to produce confusion with his false clinics. Without people being inoculated against the plain and simple truth, they would be able to see and understand. The doctrine that produces tares is a confusion of the facts, so people trust in falsehood, and think the true Gospel is not good news anymore. Notice the doctrine of the devil that the tares believed, and thus were tares and not wheat, made them "lawless". Jesus said they were workers of "anomia". They didn't think they had to obey! This was due to the devil's seed or doctrine his servants sowed! Are you listening?

71

Some of the Devil's clinics teach that our personal faith is a gift from God, and not something we have to choose and do. They get this from a misunderstanding (the Devil doesn't misunderstand) of Ephesians 2:8 where it says, *"For by grace are ye saved through **faith**; and that not of yourselves: it is the gift of God:"* Not knowing the Greek, they suppose that this passage is declaring FAITH to be the gift of God rather than SALVATION being the gift. Let us hear Adam Clarke, an acknowledged Greek scholar.

Adam Clarke: But whether are we to understand faith or salvation as being the gift of God? This question is answered by the Greek text: th gar cariti este seswsmenoi dia thv pistewv. kai touto ouk ex umwn. yeou to dwron, ouk ex ergwn. ina mh tiv kauchshtai. "By this grace ye are saved through faith; and THIS (touto, this salvation) not of you; it is the gift of God, not of works: so that no one can boast." "The relative touto, this, which is in the neuter gender, cannot stand for pistiv, faith, which is the feminine; but it has the whole sentence that goes before for its antecedent."

If faith were a gift, then every passage where Jesus upbraids his disciples for little or no faith, He is deceiving them to think that faith is somehow their responsibility. The idea that faith is a gift to the elect is just Calvinistic heresy. Faith is man's proper response to God's Light. Unbelief is man's improper response to God's Light.

Joh 1:9 *That was the true Light, which **lighteth every man** that cometh into the world....3:19 And this is the condemnation, that light is come into the world, and men loved darkness rather than light, because their deeds were evil. 20 For every one that doeth evil hateth the light, neither cometh to the light, lest his deeds should be reproved. 21 But he that doeth truth cometh to* *the light, that his deeds may be made manifest, that they are wrought in God.*

Chapter Eight

Can One Born Again Be Lost Again?

Can someone who has been born again fall away so as to perish eternally. We have already touched on the fact that the new birth is not a genetic or physical change. Is the new birth a concept of the New Testament only? If you will listen close as Jesus is speaking with Nicodemus in John chapter 3, you will find that Jesus expected Nicodemus to understand the concept of the new birth; and the only Scriptures that then existed were those of what we call the Old Testament. What did the Old Testament say about the new birth that Nicodemus should have comprehended? Everyone saved in the Old Testament had to be saved by grace through faith, which required a turning of their heart to God in faith and repentance at some time in their life. This spiritual birth into a right relationship with God is the essence of the new birth. Many times in the Old Testament God calls upon the people to circumcise their hearts, and not just their flesh (Deut 10:16 & Jer. 4:4). We know Saul was a new man when the Spirit of God came upon him, and then again was miserable when the Spirit of God left him. Listen to some passages from the Old Testament that speak of these concepts.

Ez 18:30 ¶ *Therefore I will judge you, O house of Israel, every one according to his ways, saith the Lord GOD. Repent, and turn yourselves from all your transgressions; so iniquity shall not be your ruin. 31 Cast away from you all your transgressions, whereby ye have transgressed; and* **make you a new heart and a new spirit:** *for why will ye die, O house of Israel? 32 For I have no pleasure in the death of him that dieth, saith the Lord GOD: wherefore turn yourselves, and live ye.*

Ez 36:25 *Then will I sprinkle clean water upon you, and ye shall be clean: from all your filthiness, and from all your idols, will I cleanse you. 26* **A new heart also will I give you, and a new spirit will I put within you: and I will take away the stony heart out of your flesh, and I will give you an heart of flesh.** *27* **And I will put my spirit within you,** *and cause you to walk in my statutes, and ye shall keep my judgments, and do them. 28 And ye shall dwell in the land that I gave to your fathers; and ye shall be my people, and I will be your God. 29 I will also save you from all your uncleannesses: and I will call for the corn, and will increase it, and lay no famine upon you. 30 And I will multiply the fruit of the tree, and the increase of the field, that ye shall receive no more reproach of famine among the heathen. 31* **Then shall ye remember your own evil ways, and your doings that were not good, and shall lothe yourselves in your own sight for your iniquities and for your abominations.** *32 Not for your sakes do I this, saith the Lord GOD, be it known unto you: be ashamed and confounded for your own ways, O house of Israel.*

VERSE: *37 Thus saith the Lord GOD;* **I will yet for this be enquired of by the house of Israel, to do it for them;**

God wanted the people to ask for a new heart and new spirit which would aid them in obeying God's Word and cause them to hate their old evil ways. This concept is a spiritual rebirth, and Jesus expected the Jewish leaders to understand the need for this in order to see the kingdom of God.   Listen to another Old Testament passage that outlines a spiritual rebirth:

Isa 55:7 *Let the wicked forsake his way, and the unrighteous man his thoughts: and let him return unto the LORD, and he will have mercy upon him; and to our God, for he will abundantly pardon.*

Remember that the tares were children of the wicked one by receiving the doctrine sowed by the devil. We are born again by the hearing and receiving of the Word of God as we mentioned earlier.

1Pe 1:23 *Being born again, not of corruptible seed, but of incorruptible, by the word of God, which liveth and abideth for ever.*

The term "born again" is spiritual language just like Jesus saying He was the manna from heaven.   He told the people they must eat his flesh and drink his blood, or they would have no life in them. This offended the ones who did not perceive the spiritual language; but took him literal.

I was raised in the "once saved, always saved" teaching; but after having been to their colleges and pastoring in their churches, I began studying to know the mechanics of salvation – How does it all fit and work?   When you understand the mechanics, you can no longer believe in this unconditional eternal security deception.   I learned that the place of security was clearly in abiding within the covenant God has graciously set up with His church. If you know the boundaries and conditions of this covenant, then you know when you are IN and when you are NOT.

1Pe 4:19 *Wherefore let them that suffer according to the will of God **commit the keeping of their souls to him in well doing,** as unto a faithful Creator.*

It is quite clear that the place of security is in the keeping of God's will and staying on the narrow road – "well doing". King David understood the principles of salvation, and this is why Paul quotes him in Romans 4 concerning the concept of "faith imputed for righteousness", which is the essence of salvation by grace. David understood this; but did David believe this meant he could not lose his inheritance and miss heaven? Listen to what he tells Solomon toward the end of his life.

1Ch 28:9 *And thou, Solomon my son, know thou the God of thy father, and serve him with a perfect heart and with a willing mind: for the LORD searcheth all hearts, and understandeth all the imaginations of the thoughts: **if thou seek him, he will be found of thee; but if thou forsake him, he will cast thee off for ever.***

Paul and Peter both say that the Old Testament prophets understood salvation by grace through faith. Paul's famous quotation, "the just shall live by faith" comes from Habakkuk 2:4 (See also Acts 10:43; 24:14; Ro 1:2; I Pe 1:10). Did the prophets and priests then believe in an unconditional eternal security?

2Ch 15:2 *And he went out to meet Asa, and said unto him, Hear ye me, Asa, and all Judah and Benjamin; The LORD is with you, while ye be with him; and if ye seek him, he will be found of you; but if ye forsake him, he will forsake you.*

Ezr 8:22 *For I was ashamed to require of the king a band of soldiers and horsemen to help us against the enemy in the way: because we had spoken unto the king, saying, The hand of our*

God is upon all them for good that seek him; but his power and his wrath is against all them that forsake him.

Ez 33:13 *When I shall say to the righteous, **that he shall surely live**; if he trust to his own righteousness, and commit iniquity, all his righteousnesses shall not be remembered; but for his iniquity that he hath committed, he shall die for it. 14 Again, when I say unto the wicked, Thou shalt surely die; if he turn from his sin, and do that which is lawful and right; 15 If the wicked restore the pledge, give again that he had robbed, walk in the statutes of life, without committing iniquity; he shall surely live, he shall not die. 16 None of his sins that he hath committed shall be mentioned unto him: he hath done that which is lawful and right; he shall surely live. 17 Yet the children of thy people say, The way of the Lord is not equal: but as for them, **their way is not equal.** 18 When the righteous turneth from his righteousness, and committeth iniquity, **he shall even die thereby.** 19 But if the wicked turn from his wickedness, and do that which is lawful and right, **he shall live thereby.***

If you believe you cannot be rejected of God once you have a born again experience, then your ways are not equal according to the Word of the Lord through Ezekiel. Just because you find a verse that says the righteous will *SURELY LIVE* this does not mean that when he rebels or grows cold, he will still be saved.

Let me share some obvious and undeniable passages which teach that those who were once on their way to heaven can be lost, and again be on their way to hell. Put aside whatever prejudices you have been indoctrinated with and simply ask yourself, "What does the Bible say?"

#1 *Matt 18:32* *Then his lord, after that he had called him, said unto him, O thou wicked servant, I forgave thee all that debt, because thou desiredst me: 33 Shouldest not thou also have had compassion on thy fellowservant, even as I had pity on thee? 34 And his lord was wroth, and delivered him to the tormentors, till he should pay all that was due unto him. 35 **So likewise shall my heavenly Father do also unto you, if ye from your hearts forgive not every one his brother their trespasses.***

We have mentioned this passage previously, so I won't linger here; but observe that this man's forgiveness was revoked. He had at one time been forgiven of his debt; but now he has to pay it. Jesus says as plain as possible that this could happen to...who? The disciples that he is speaking to!

#2 *Matt 24:12* *And because iniquity shall abound, the love of many shall wax cold. 13 But he that shall endure unto the end, the same shall be saved.*

Consider the obvious: If you have love that waxed cold, then at one time it was hot. The reason the person didn't endure to the end and be saved is because his love waxed cold; which means he would have been alright had this not happened. If his love had **not** waxed cold, then he **would** have been saved; but it **did** wax cold, so he would **not** be saved. If I told my children they could have a cookie **if** they finished their supper, then I've also told them that if they **don't** finish their supper, they will **not** get a cookie. There is no way to get away from the simple and perspicuous import of the passage without getting into the realm of twisting and wresting the Scripture from it obvious meaning.

#3 *Luke 8:13* *They on the rock are they, which, when they hear, receive the word with joy; and these have no root, which for a while believe, and in time of temptation fall away.*

Jesus clearly said they received the Word with joy and believed. If they had continued in this state they would have been saved, otherwise there is really no meaning to the passage at all. They came into a state where they would have been saved had they continued in that state; but they fell away from that position. They could not fall away from a place they had never been. If they never really were IN, then they couldn't fall OUT. The reason they fell away from a safe state, is because they had no root, and therefore they didn't continue unto salvation. Some try to say, "They had a superficial belief" – Then what was wrong with falling away from that? To continue in that would have been terrible. That is not what the passage is trying to teach; but rather that they SHOULD have continued; but DIDN'T.

#4 *Jn 15:1* *I am the true vine, and my Father is the husbandman. 2 Every branch in me that beareth not fruit he taketh away: and every branch that beareth fruit, he purgeth it, that it may bring forth more fruit. 3 Now ye are clean through the word which I have spoken unto you. 4* **Abide** *in me, and I in you. As the branch cannot bear fruit of itself, except it* **abide** *in the vine; no more can ye, except ye* **abide** *in me. 5 I am the vine, ye are the branches: He that* **abideth** *in me, and I in him, the same bringeth forth much fruit: for without me ye can do nothing. 6 If a man* **abide not** *in me, he is cast forth as a branch, and is withered; and men gather them, and cast them into the fire, and they are burned. 7 If ye* **abide** *in me, and my words* **abide** *in you, ye shall ask what ye will, and it shall be done unto you. 8 Herein is my Father glorified, that ye bear* *much fruit; so shall ye be my disciples. 9 ¶ As the Father hath loved me, so have I loved you:* **continue** *ye in my love. 10 If ye keep my commandments, ye shall* **abide** *in my love; even as I have kept my Father's commandments, and* **abide** *in his love.*

You will notice that I have emboldened a number of words. These words are all from the same Greek word, "Meno", which means to "remain", "abide", "continue", etc. This little word is seen in I Jn 2:24 in all three of these meanings.

I Jn 2:24 Let that therefore **abide** *in you, which ye have heard from the beginning. If that which ye have heard from the beginning shall* **remain** *in you, ye also shall* **continue** *in the Son, and in the Father. 25 And this is the promise that he hath promised us, even eternal life.*

It is obvious to the unbiased mind that John believed you must remain in Christ by having his words remaining in you. If His words did not remain in you in the sense of you adhering to them, then you would not continue or remain in Christ; and consequently would not receive the promise of eternal life. It is very clear from John 15 that Jesus wasn't teaching unconditional security; but showing that if they didn't bear fruit, they would be cut off and cast away. This meant they would not continue or remain in His love! There is no unconditional love here! You have the life of the vine in you while you are connected to the vine -- "He that hath the Son, hath life". When you are disconnected from the vine, you wither because the life of Christ is not flowing into you any more. You are then lost and cast into the fire. The term "abide in Christ" isn't some mystical deeper Christian experience; but a very practical "staying or remaining or continuing within the boundaries of a conditional covenant relationship with Christ". Listen to John again with the same compelling message.

2Jo 9 *Whosoever **transgresseth**, and **abideth not** in the **doctrine of Christ**, hath not God. He that **abideth** in the **doctrine of Christ**, he hath both the Father and the Son.*

#5 *Rom 8:1* *There is therefore now no condemnation to them which are in Christ Jesus, who walk not after the flesh, but after the Spirit. 2 For the law of the Spirit of life in Christ Jesus hath made me free from the law of sin and death. 3 For what the law could not do, in that it was weak through the flesh, God sending his own Son in the likeness of sinful flesh, and for sin, condemned sin in the flesh: 4 That the righteousness of the law might be fulfilled in us, who walk not after the flesh, but after the Spirit. 5 For they that are after the flesh do mind the things of the flesh; but they that are after the Spirit the things of the Spirit. 6 For to be carnally minded is death; but to be spiritually minded is life and peace. 7 Because the carnal mind is enmity against God: for it is not subject to the law of God, neither indeed can be. 8 So then they that are in the flesh cannot please God. 9 But ye are not in the flesh, but in the Spirit, if so be that the Spirit of God dwell in you. Now if any man have not the Spirit of Christ, he is none of his. 10 And if Christ be in you, the body is dead because of sin; but the Spirit is life because of righteousness. 11 But if the Spirit of him that raised up Jesus from the dead dwell in you, he that raised up Christ from the dead shall also quicken your mortal bodies by his Spirit that dwelleth in you. 12 **Therefore, brethren, we are debtors, not to the flesh, to live after the flesh. 13 For if ye live after the flesh, ye shall die: but if ye through the Spirit do mortify the deeds of the body, ye shall live. 14 For as many as are led by the Spirit of God, they are the sons of God.***

The apostle tells us that our life is dependent upon us mortifying the deeds of the body, rather than living after the flesh. With all the Lord has done for us, and with the Spirit of Christ residing in us, we are not debtors to the flesh, to live after the flesh; but if we, notwithstanding all the Lord has done for us, yet choose to live after the flesh WE SHALL DIE. Walking in the Spirit and being led of the Spirit are essential to maintain spiritual life. This warning and exhortation was to believers; and those who really care to know the truth can see clearly the danger. We have a similar conditional situation presented in the passage below. We must maintain our relationship with God.

2 Cor. 6:17 *Wherefore come out from among them, and be ye separate, saith the Lord, and touch not the unclean thing; and I will receive you, 18 And will be a Father unto you, and ye shall be my sons and daughters, saith the Lord Almighty 7:1 Having therefore these promises (conditions), dearly beloved, let us cleanse ourselves from all filthiness of the flesh and spirit, perfecting holiness in the fear of God.*

#6 *Rom11:17* *And if some of the branches be broken off, and thou, being a wild olive tree, wert graffed in among them, and with them partakest of the root and fatness of the olive tree; 18 Boast not against the branches. But if thou boast, thou bearest not the root, but the root thee. 19 Thou wilt say then, The branches were broken off, that I might be graffed in. 20 Well;* ***because of unbelief they were broken off,*** *and* ***thou standest by faith.*** *Be not highminded, but fear: 21 For if God spared not the natural branches, take heed lest he also spare not thee. 22* ***Behold therefore the goodness and severity of God: on them which fell, severity; but toward thee, goodness, if thou continue in his goodness: otherwise thou also shalt be cut off.***

This passage is about as plain as it can get! The Jews who didn't accept Christ were cut off from the vine of God's salvation. Believing Gentiles were grafted into the vine of God's salvation; but had better not be presumptuous about their new position. They stood by faith in God's grace; but they had better continue in that faith, or they would be cut off just like those unbelieving Jews were. There is no way to get around this clear warning. Those who try to say this passage is speaking nationally to Jews and Gentiles simply need a head examination. All Jews were never cut off, and all Gentiles were never grafted in. Only the unbelieving Jews (branches – plural) were broken off, and only believing Gentiles were grafted in (Acts 10 & 15). We are clearly dealing with individuals who stand by faith and must continue in God's goodness or be cut off from the vine into which they were grafted.

#7 *Rom 14:15* *But if thy brother be grieved with thy meat, now walkest thou not charitably. Destroy not him with thy meat, for whom Christ died.*

Also: *1Co 8:11* *And through thy knowledge shall the weak brother perish, for whom Christ died?*

These potent warnings from the apostle must not be overlooked. Consider what Adam Clarke says on the passages:

Clarke: From this verse we learn that a man for whom Christ died may perish, or have his soul destroyed; and destroyed with such a destruction as implies perdition; the original is very emphatic, mh-ekeinon apollue, uper ou cristov apeyane. Christ died in his stead; do not destroy his soul. The sacrificial death is as strongly expressed as it can be, and there is no word in the New Testament that more forcibly implies eternal ruin than the verb apolluw, from which is derived that most significant name of the Devil, o apolluwn, the DESTROYER, the great universal murderer of souls.

The apostle would be wrong to bring in the fact that Christ died for this person, if the "destroying" he is speaking of would have no affect on that point. Christ dying to save his soul, and you destroying his once converted soul is clearly the issue at hand.

#8 *1Cor. 9:23 And this I do for the gospel's sake, **that I might be partaker thereof with you**. 24 Know ye not that they which run in a race run all, but one receiveth the prize? So run, that ye may obtain. 25 And every man that striveth for the mastery is temperate in all things. Now they do it to obtain a corruptible crown; but we an incorruptible. 26 I therefore so run, not as uncertainly; so fight I, not as one that beateth the air: 27 But I keep under my body, and bring it into subjection: lest that by any means, when I have preached to others, **I myself should be a castaway.***

*10:1 ¶ Moreover, brethren, I would not that ye should be ignorant, how that **all** our fathers were under the cloud, and **all** passed through the sea; 2 And were **all baptized** unto Moses in the cloud and in the sea; 3 And did **all eat the same spiritual meat**; 4 And did **all drink the same spiritual drink**: for they drank of that spiritual Rock that followed them: and that **Rock was Christ**. 5 But with many of them God was not well pleased: **for they were overthrown in the wilderness.** 6 ¶ Now these things were **our examples**, to the intent we should not lust after evil things, as they also lusted. 7 Neither be ye idolaters, as were some of them; as it is written, The people sat down to eat and drink, and rose up to play. 8 Neither let us commit fornication, as some of them committed, and fell in one day three and twenty thousand. 9 Neither let us tempt Christ, as some of them also tempted, and were destroyed of serpents. 10 Neither murmur ye, as some of them also murmured, and were* *destroyed of the destroyer. 11 **Now all these things happened unto them for ensamples**: and they are written for our admonition, upon whom the ends of the world are come. 12 **Wherefore let him that thinketh he standeth take heed lest he fall.**

Could the Apostle speak with more clarity? First Paul tells them that his striving is so that he might be a partaker of the gospel with them (9:23); then he proceeds to explain his meaning in the remainder of chapter nine. After stating clearly that he himself could be a castaway if he didn't "mortify the deeds of the body" (Remember Romans 8); he explains with an example from the Old Testament. The clear and undeniable point is that ALL the fathers had the SAME thing when they started out. They ALL had the SAME baptism, and ALL partook of the SAME spiritual meat and drink, which is clearly said to be Christ. The point is that though all started out with the **same** "new birth", many were overthrown and were not ultimately saved. Paul clearly sums up the matter by saying, "**Wherefore let him that thinketh he standeth take heed lest he fall.**"

I hope you are paying close attention; because he is speaking to us about not being presumptuous about our "standing". Who was Paul warning? Why was he warning them? Paul makes it plain that he was striving to attain unto the resurrection of the just, which is ultimate salvation – the end of the narrow path.

Php 3:10 *That I may know him, and the power of his resurrection, and the fellowship of his sufferings, being made conformable unto his death; 11 **If by any means I might attain unto the resurrection of the dead.** 12 Not as though I had already attained, either were already perfect: but I follow after,* *if that I may apprehend that for which also I am apprehended of Christ Jesus. 13 Brethren, I count not myself to have apprehended: but this one thing I do, forgetting those things which are behind, and reaching forth unto those things which are before, 14 I press toward the mark for the prize of the high calling of God in Christ Jesus.*

The prize of the high calling of God was ultimate salvation – the crown of life – the resurrection of the dead – that for which he was apprehended of Christ and was thus striving to apprehend.

#9 *Gal 6:7 Be not deceived; God is not mocked: for whatsoever a man soweth, that shall he also reap. 8 For he that soweth to his flesh shall of the flesh reap corruption;* **but he that soweth to the Spirit shall of the Spirit reap life everlasting.** *9 And let us not be weary in well doing: for in due season we shall reap,* **if we faint not.**

If we sow to the Spirit we will reap life everlasting, IF WE FAINT NOT. What if we faint or start sowing to the flesh?? Only two possible things could happen; either God will be mocked, or we will NOT inherit eternal life. Since we know God will not be mocked, then we surely know that we will reap corruption and not eternal life. Corruption is obviously meant to be antithetical to life everlasting. The message is plain enough.

#10 *2 Tim2:11 It is a faithful saying: For if we be dead with him, we shall also live with him: 12 If we suffer, we shall also reign with him:* **if we deny him, he also will deny us:** *13 If we believe not, yet he abideth faithful: he cannot deny himself.*

Surely everyone knows that Paul and Timothy were genuinely converted disciples; but what is this that Paul says to Timothy? There was an ongoing obligation to be faithful to Christ to the end in order to be accepted of Him. See this clearly in *2 Cor. 5:9* *Wherefore we labour, that, whether present or absent, we may be accepted of him.* Listen to what else Paul says to Timothy:

I Tim 4:16 *Take heed unto thyself, and unto the doctrine; continue in them: for in doing this thou shalt both* **save thyself, and them that hear thee.**

Didn't Paul believe that Timothy was already "saved"? Paul believed Timothy was genuinely converted to Christ; but salvation ultimately comes at the end of the narrow way, remember?

#11 *Heb 2:1* *Therefore we ought to give the more earnest heed to the things which we have heard, lest at any time we should let them slip. 2 For if the word spoken by angels was stedfast, and every transgression and disobedience received a just recompence of reward; 3* **How shall we escape,** *if we neglect so great salvation; which at the first began to be spoken by the Lord, and was confirmed unto us by them that heard him;*

There is a theme that runs through the book of Hebrews. It is a strong warning against apostasy. Some have vainly attempted to say it is warning people to "make sure they really got it"; but any intelligent reader can see that the warnings are to "hold fast" what they already had. If they didn't already have IT, they certainly would not want to hold fast that which they had. Hebrews 2:1 is the first of many "therefore" and "wherefore" passages which give an earnest appeal to continue in the faith. These appeals are to believers who are members of the Christian church, and they are clearly warned to be steadfast and hold fast their faith. Listen close.

#12 *Heb 3:6 But Christ as a son over his own house; whose house are we, **if we hold fast the confidence and the rejoicing of the hope firm unto the end.** 7 Wherefore (as the Holy Ghost saith, To day if ye will hear his voice, 8 Harden not your hearts, as in the provocation, in the day of temptation in the wilderness: 9 When your fathers tempted me, proved me, and saw my works forty years. 10 Wherefore I was grieved with that generation, and said, They do alway err in their heart; and they have not known my ways. 11 So I sware in my wrath, They shall not enter into my rest.) 12 **Take heed, brethren, lest there be in any of you an evil heart of unbelief, in departing from the living God. 13 But exhort one another daily, while it is called To day; lest any of you be hardened through the deceitfulness of sin. 14 For we are made partakers of Christ, if we hold the beginning of our confidence stedfast unto the end;***

Here we find the same illustration Paul gave in I Corinthians 10 of the people God saved out of Egypt being so uncooperative that God refused to take them on into the promised land. There is an unambiguous warning that those whose love is waxing cold are heading straight toward a "cut off", where God will stop being gracious because it is no longer appropriate in this case. The warning is to believers who have been delivered from "Egypt" to not harden their hearts or provoke God lest they not enter into the Promised Land i.e. Heaven. It clearly says we are made partakers of Christ IF we hold the beginning of our confidence or faith steadfast unto the end of our journey. In Hebrews chapter four Paul continues this thought and exhorts that we **labor** to enter into our rest – the promised land – heaven. The warning surfaces again to these very people who were Christians long enough to be teachers, but instead were still babes, because they were dull of hearing, i.e. they were not keeping pace with the exhortations they received. Paul sees this as dangerous, thus the next warning:

#13 *Heb 6:1 Therefore leaving the principles of the doctrine of Christ, let us go on unto perfection; not laying again the foundation of repentance from dead works, and of faith toward God, 2 Of the doctrine of baptisms, and of laying on of hands, and of resurrection of the dead, and of eternal judgment. 3 And this will we do,* ***if God permit****. 4 For it is* ***impossible*** *for those who were once enlightened, and have tasted of the heavenly gift, and were made partakers of the Holy Ghost, 5 And have tasted the good word of God, and the powers of the world to come, 6* ***If they shall fall away, to renew them again unto repentance****; seeing they crucify to themselves the Son of God afresh, and put him to an open shame. 7 For the earth which drinketh in the rain that cometh oft upon it, and bringeth forth herbs meet for them by whom it is dressed, receiveth blessing from God: 8 But that which beareth thorns and briers is rejected, and is nigh unto cursing;* ***whose end is to be burned.*** *9 But, beloved, we are persuaded better things of you, and things that accompany salvation, though we thus speak. 10 For God is not unrighteous to forget your work and labour of love, which ye have shewed toward his name, in that ye have ministered to the saints, and do minister. 11 And we desire that every one of you do shew the* ***same diligence to the full assurance of hope unto the end****: 12 That ye be not slothful, but followers of* ***them who through faith and patience inherit the promises.*** *13 For when God made promise to Abraham, because he could swear by no greater, he sware by himself, 14 Saying, Surely blessing I will bless thee, and multiplying I will multiply thee. 15 And so,* ***after he had patiently endured, he obtained the promise.***

Why would not God permit someone to go on to perfection? If someone has received all the grace God offers in conversion that is listed here, yet __turns away__ from Christ (The Greek is not passive) and rejoins those who

91

rejected Christ, thus crucifying to himself the Son of God afresh, and putting Him to open shame; God will not permit him to go on to the promised land, but cuts him off from the vine and casts him away. Having hardened his heart through the deceitfulness of sin to the point of turning his back on Christ, it is now impossible for him to repent. God's Spirit is no longer working with him; and he has been sent strong delusion as spoken of in 2 Thess. 2:11,12. Remember Rom. 11:22; I Co 10; John 15; etc.? This cogent warning again surfaces in Hebrews chapter ten.

#14 *Heb 10:26 For if we sin wilfully after that we have received the knowledge of the truth, there remaineth no more sacrifice for sins, 27 But a certain fearful looking for of judgment and fiery indignation, which shall devour the adversaries. 28 He that despised Moses' law died without mercy under two or three witnesses: 29 Of how much sorer punishment, suppose ye, shall he be thought worthy, who hath trodden under foot the Son of God, and hath counted the blood of the covenant, wherewith he was sanctified, an unholy thing, and hath done despite unto the Spirit of grace?*

Here the apostle is sounding the same alarm to those who might turn away from the path of righteousness to willful sin. If they do this, there is no other path of forgiveness or atonement. The blood of bulls and goats cannot do it; so Judaism is not an option for salvation apart from Jesus Christ as the Lamb of God. This passage is referencing off the same principle that applied in the Old Testament, and Paul is directly referring to what happened in Numbers chapter fifteen when a man willfully disobeyed the Law of Moses. He died without mercy because he despised the Word of the Lord. In the New Testament we have a greater covenant and therefore we are more accountable with "sorer" consequences when we trample under foot God's Son. Paul says this man who did this had been sanctified by the blood of the covenant; so there is no denying that he was born again, and on his way to heaven previous to his rebellion. Having a sorer punishment than "dying without mercy" is certainly not spoken of a man still on his way to heaven. This is just another warning to continue in the faith, and when put together with the other warnings in Hebrews, it should put the fear of God in any presumptuous soul trusting in an unconditional security teaching.

For the sake of time and space I will not quote all of Hebrews twelve; but these lucid warnings surface there again. We are clearly told that if we faint at or despise the chastening of the Lord, we will die spiritually, *"shall we not much rather be in subjection unto the Father of spirits, and* **live***?"* This is in the context of failing of the grace of God like Esau who sold his birthright for a mess of pottage. This we are in danger of doing, if we sell our inheritance for earthly pleasure or reprieve from persecution, as these believers were troubled with. The very reason for all the warnings is because they were suffering great persecution. The apostle sums up all these warnings toward the end of this chapter when he says, *"See that ye refuse not him that speaketh. For if they escaped not who refused him that spake on earth (Moses), much more shall not we escape, if we turn away from him that speaketh from heaven (Jesus):"*

#15 *Jas 5:19* Brethren, if any of you do err from the truth, and one convert him; 20 Let him know, that he which converteth the sinner from the error of his way shall save a soul from death, and shall hide a multitude of sins.

If a brother is led away (passive in the Greek) with erroneous doctrine, and a faithful brother converts him back to the truth before it is too late, he will save a soul from DEATH, and hide a multitude of sins by bringing him back under the blood of the covenant. This soul was in LIFE, but it could again be in death, and cut off eternally - just like Romans 8:13 teaches. This brother was headed for a "cut-off"; but another brother graciously turned him around. Consider the relationship of this passage with Mt 18:15 *"...thou has gained thy brother"*; which is much more preferable than the other possible outcome in Mt 18:17.

#16 *2Pe 1:10 Wherefore the rather, brethren, give diligence to make your calling and election sure: for **if ye do these things**, ye shall **never fall**: 11 For so an **entrance shall be ministered unto you** abundantly into the everlasting kingdom of our Lord and Saviour Jesus Christ.*

Can you see the obvious? Election is not definite and unchangeable, nor unconditional; but we have to continue in the faith to make our calling and election SURE. **If** we **do** the things that Peter has exhorted us to do in the first part of the chapter, we will never fall. **If** we **don't fall,** then an entrance shall be given us into the everlasting Kingdom of Christ. SO...What **if** we **don't** do the things Peter tells us and we **do fall**? Then we will **NOT** have an entrance into the everlasting Kingdom of Christ.

#17 *2Pe 2:20 For if after they have escaped the pollutions of the world through the knowledge of the Lord and Saviour Jesus Christ, they are again entangled therein, and overcome, the **latter end is worse** with them than the beginning. 21 For it had been better for them not to have known the way of*

94

righteousness, than, after they have known it, to turn from the holy commandment delivered unto them. 22 But it is happened unto them according to the true proverb, The dog is turned to his own vomit again; and the sow that was washed to her wallowing in the mire.

This verse is proof positive that souls on their way to heaven can be lost and go to hell or words mean nothing. These people were on their way to heaven; but were entangled and overcome. If this had not happened, they would have made it to heaven; but because this happened, their latter end is now worse than the beginning. How? Because they would have been better off not to have heard the gospel than to turn away from Christ after knowing Him.

If they were never on their way to heaven, then from what did they escape, and how can it be said they were entangled again and overcome? **Would this man have been alright had he NOT been entangled again and overcome? Would he have been saved had he NOT returned to the mire?** If he would have still gone to hell, then what is the purpose of all this? If he was on the narrow road that leads to life, and we know he was; is he then now on his way to hell? He must be, or else how can his latter end be worse than the beginning before he was even preached too. The only answer is that an apostate who has enjoyed the blessing of conversion, but turns back is under greater judgment; which is exactly what Hebrews tells us.

It says the sow was *washed*; but what would this refer to, if the man was not washed in the blood? You say, "But it calls him a sow, not a sheep"; yes, and Peter and Jesus call lost men "sheep going astray" too. You cannot build doctrine on types and symbols. A man who escaped the pollutions of the world through Jesus Christ and was "Washed"; but then was AGAIN entangled and overcome so that his latter end was worse than the beginning can only mean one thing!

#18 *Jude 3 Beloved, when I gave all diligence to write unto you of the common salvation, it was needful for me to write unto you, and exhort you that ye should earnestly contend for the faith which was once delivered unto the saints. 4 For there are certain men crept in unawares, who were before of old ordained to this condemnation, ungodly men, turning the grace of our God into lasciviousness, and denying the only Lord God, and our Lord Jesus Christ. 5* **I will therefore put you in remembrance, though ye once knew this, how that the Lord, having saved the people out of the land of Egypt, afterward destroyed them that believed not.**

Those who turn the grace of God into lasciviousness or "lack of restraint" i.e. no law, no rules, no obedience, etc; are the same ones who teach you cannot fall away through sin; but listen to what Jude speaks of. He speaks of the same illustration that Paul uses in 1Co 10 and throughout Hebrews. That after the people were SAVED out of Egypt, God afterwards destroyed those who didn't **"hold the beginning of [their] confidence stedfast unto the end;"** These men are described as "Twice Dead" and "plucked up by the roots". How could they be twice dead, if they had never been converted or "alive" at one time? Jude exhorts the believers at the end, **"Keep yourselves in the love of God, looking for the mercy of our Lord Jesus Christ unto eternal life."** What does all this mean? Just the same as all the other passages we have been discussing; but we are not finished.

#19 _Rev 2:7_ He that hath an ear, let him hear what the Spirit saith unto the churches; **To him that overcometh will I give to eat of the tree of life**, which is in the midst of the paradise of God.

_2:10_ Fear none of those things which thou shalt suffer: behold, the devil shall cast some of you into prison, that ye may be tried; and ye shall have tribulation ten days: be thou faithful unto death, and I will give thee a crown of life. 11 He that hath an ear, let him hear what the Spirit saith unto the churches; **He that overcometh shall not be hurt of the second death.**

_2:17_ He that hath an ear, let him hear what the Spirit saith unto the churches; **To him that overcometh** will I give to eat of the hidden manna, and will give him a white stone, and in the stone a new name written, which no man knoweth saving he that receiveth it.

_2:26_ And **he that overcometh, and keepeth my works unto the end**, to him will I give power over the nations:

_3:5_ **He that overcometh**, the same shall be clothed in white raiment; and **I will not blot out his name out of the book of life,** but I will confess his name before my Father, and before his angels. 6 He that hath an ear, let him hear what the Spirit saith unto the churches.

_3:21_ **To him that overcometh** will I grant to sit with me in my throne, even as I also overcame, and am set down with my Father in his throne.

_21:6_ And he said unto me, It is done. I am Alpha and Omega, the beginning and the end. I will give unto him that is athirst of the fountain of the water of life freely. 7 **He that overcometh** shall inherit all things; and **I will be his God,** and **he shall be my son**. 8 But the fearful, and unbelieving, and the abominable, and murderers, and whoremongers, and sorcerers, and idolaters, and all liars, shall have their part in the lake which burneth with fire and brimstone: which is the second death.

_22:14_ Blessed are they that **do his commandments**, that they may have right to the tree of life, and **may enter in through the gates into the city**.

"If you finish your dinner, you may have a cookie." What does this mean? It means, **"If you <u>don't</u> finish your meal you <u>cannot</u> have a cookie"**. If you do not overcome and keep his works unto the end, you **will** be blotted out of the book of life, and **will** be hurt of the second death. Common sense is a must if you wish to understand God's Word – something that theologians are often lacking. Don't gamble your eternal soul on some man's efforts to avoid the obvious import of God's clear Word. You will be held accountable before God for what the Bible actually says! Where is the place of security and salvation in these weighty and compelling passages?

Chapter Nine

What Is The Book Of Life?

I've heard many theories about what the book of life is, and what it means to have your name put in or blotted out of the book of life. Usually people are looking to defend their false security, so they are grasping for some explanation that helps them avoid the obvious. The book of life is God's roll book. When the roll is called up yonder, will you be there? Will your name be there? This is the issue. If you look at all the passages in the Bible that speak of the Book of life, you will see it is a roll book of God's saints. Lets look at them.

Ex 32:32 *Yet now, if thou wilt forgive their sin--;* ***and if not, blot me, I pray thee, out of thy book which thou hast written.*** *33 And the LORD said unto Moses, Whosoever hath sinned against me,* ***him will I blot out of my book.***

What is obvious? Moses was in the book, but realized that when men sin beyond what God will forgive, they are blotted out. If they are forgiven, they are not blotted out. Moses is offering to be a sacrifice for the people; but God says he will only blot out those whom He will not forgive in this situation.

Php 4:3 *And I intreat thee also, true yokefellow, help those women which laboured with me in the gospel, with Clement*

*also, and with other my fellowlabourers, **whose names are in
the book of life.***

The Apostle Paul is commending certain brothers and
sisters to the church leaders at Philippi. In commending
them as true believers, he states his confidence that their
names are in the book of life. This would mean nothing if
all living people had their name in the book of life as some
people imagine.

Re 3:5 *He that overcometh, the same shall be clothed in white
raiment; and **I will not blot out his name out of the book of life**,
but I will confess his name before my Father, and before his
angels.*

Is this consistent with what we have already seen? Of
course it is, the Bible is always consistent. If we continue
in the covenant God has established with the church, then
we are safe; but if we fail to continue, then we are sinning
willfully, and there remaineth no more sacrifice for sin. If
we don't continue and hold fast the beginning of our
confidence steadfast unto the end, then we will not be
partakers of Christ; but rather our names will be blotted
out of His roll book. If we overcome, Jesus will confess
our name before His Father and before the holy angels.
This verse is closely related to the one below:

Mark 8:34 *And when he had called the people unto him with
his disciples also, he said unto them, Whosoever will come after
me, let him deny himself, and take up his cross, and follow me.
35 For whosoever will save his life shall lose it; but whosoever
shall lose his life for my sake and the gospel's, the same shall
save it. 36 For what shall it profit a man, if he shall gain the
whole world, and lose his own soul? 37 Or what shall a man
give in exchange for his soul? 38 Whosoever therefore shall be
ashamed of me and of my words in this adulterous and sinful*

*generation; **of him also shall the Son of man be ashamed, when he cometh in the glory of his Father with the holy angels.***

***Re 13:8** And all that dwell upon the earth shall worship him, **whose names are not written in the book of life** of the Lamb slain from the foundation of the world.*

Those who worship the beast are not the followers of Jesus, and this is stated by saying their names are not in His book.

***Re 17:8** The beast that thou sawest was, and is not; and shall ascend out of the bottomless pit, and go into perdition: and they that dwell on the earth shall wonder, whose **names were not written in the book of life** from the foundation of the world, when they behold the beast that was, and is not, and yet is.*

Again, all those who wonder after the beast are lost men, whose names are not in the Lamb's book of life.

Re 20:12** And I saw the dead, small and great, stand before God; and the books were opened: and another book was opened, **which is the book of life:** and the dead were judged out of those things which were written in the books, according to their works....15 And **whosoever was not found written in the book of life was cast into the lake of fire.

Again this is consistent with the facts already seen. When you become the Lord's child, your name is written in His roll book; but if you forsake Him, your name is blotted out, and you receive no inheritance with the saints.

***Re 21:27** And there shall in no wise enter into it any thing that defileth, neither whatsoever worketh abomination, or* *maketh a lie:* **but they which are written in the Lamb's book of life.**

This would mean nothing if all living people were in the book of life, but only blotted out when they rejected Jesus, as some erroneously teach. What about those who never heard about Jesus? Are they automatically saved? If so, we'd be better off not to preach or send out missionaries.   Only the children of God are in the book of life.

Re 22:19 *And if any man shall take away from the words of the book of this prophecy, God shall take away his part out of the book of life, and out of the holy city, and from the things which are written in this book.*

This is a grave warning, and proves that one who was truly a child of God, and on his way to heaven, can so offend that he will be cut off and blotted out of the book of life to be damned with other lost men. Friend, don't run from the truth, but embrace it, and preach it, and be saved by it!

Chapter Ten

That He Might Be Just And The Justifier

Rom 3:25 *"Whom God hath* **set forth** *to be a propitiation through faith in his blood, to declare his* **[God's]** *righteousness for the remission of sins that are past* **[Genesis to Christ]**, *through the forbearance of God; 26 To declare, I say, at this time his* **[God's]** *righteousness:* ***that he [God] might be just, and the justifier of him which believeth in Jesus."***

God never cuts corners on righteousness and justice. He would never justify one sinner unless He could be JUST in doing so. Unlike fallen man, God's Law is his own love, desire, and nature. It is not something that regulates Him, but is His very opinion and preference. As said earlier, He is the master of appropriateness; and hates that which is lawless and inappropriate. The Crucifixion of Jesus Christ was a public display of God's attitude toward man's sin. Without such an awful display, God could never pardon one sinner, lest he be thought to sympathize with sin or sinners - Lest his hatred for sin, and love for holiness come into question - Lest some should think he didn't fully agree with His Law, or thought it was too harsh, etc.

In establishing government and upholding law and order, a just and righteous governor is pledged to duly administer laws in support of public order, in support of public morals, and to reward the innocent and punish those who violate the law. Every time someone violates the law, the innocent, law abiding citizens are damaged, thus, the governor is committed to upholding the law for the sake of society as a whole. God is love. God's government is the ultimate in the appropriate administration of justice, love, mercy, and grace.

Charles Finney shares that there is an important difference between retributive justice, and public justice. This same distinction is seen between the Letter of the law and the Spirit of the law or between Law and Grace. Retributive justice demands punishment without exception in order to uphold the honor and obedience due to the law for the protection of the public interests. Public justice allows mercy or pardon on the condition that something else be done that upholds and supports law and order as effectively as the execution of the law would do. Both of these are based on LOVE when executed appropriately in the wisdom and righteousness of God.

The design of legal penalties is to secure respect and obedience to the law. The same is also the reason for executing penalties when the law is violated. The penalties are to be regarded as an expression of the views of the lawgiver, in respect to the importance of his law. His execution of the penalties reveals his sincerity, commitment, and determination to abide by the principles of his government. The execution of the penalties reveals his abhorrence for all crime, and his love for his faithful law abiding subjects. The execution of the penalties shows his unalterable determination to carry out, support and establish the authority and righteousness of his laws. The execution of the penalties proves his perfect satisfaction and agreement with His Laws – He does not think they are too hard or asking too much.

It is a fact well established by experience of all ages and nations, that the exercise of mercy, in setting aside the execution of penalties, is a matter of extreme delicacy and danger. The influence of law, as might be expected, is found very much to depend upon the certainty felt by the subjects that it will be duly executed. The exercise of mercy has always been found to weaken government by begetting and fostering a hope of exemption, second chance, or escape from the penalties of the law in the minds of those who are tempted to violate the law. I say, it always weakens law and order unless a sufficient atonement is made as a substitute for the execution of the penalties of the law on the offender.

WHAT IS a sufficient ATONEMENT? Since the head of government is pledged to protect and promote the public interests by a due administration of law, if in any instance where the law is violated, he would set aside the execution of the penalties, public justice requires that a substitute for the execution of the law is provided, or that something is done that **will as effectually** secure the influence of law, as the execution of the penalty would have done. He cannot make exceptions to the spirit of the law – Either the soul that sinneth must surely die, according to the letter of the law and retributive justice; or a substitute must be provided in accordance with the spirit of the law and public justice.

The conditions of an acceptable atonement are as follows: Whatever will as fully express the Lawgiver's regard for his law, His determination to support it, His abhorrence of all violations of its precepts, and will as effectually guard against the idea that violators might escape without punishment, as the execution of the penalty would do **is a full satisfaction of public justice, and qualifies for an atonement.** This propitiates God, the Law-giver and governor, and justifies His pardon and rehabilitation of the offenders. Jesus' sacrifice AND His priestly administration to rehabilitate the sinner along with the repentant sinner's full cooperation are required to ultimately save a soul.

When these conditions are fulfilled, the lawgiver's regard for his law is upheld; His determination to support it is manifested; His abhorrence for sin is expressed; the danger to violators is as clearly displayed so that sinners thoroughly <u>repent and return to obedience</u>...then and only then is it safe to pardon and extend mercy, because by Christ's atonement, public justice and the spirit of the law have been upheld and not undermined. **The life, teachings, crucifixion, Lordship, and Priesthood of Jesus Christ so fully display God's love for his law, his hatred of sin, His determination to uphold law and order, and his unwillingness to compromise with sin, that it opens the door for Him to safely pardon repentant sinners in Jesus' name, and ultimately save them if they continued in a repentant state under the rehabilitation program Christ is administering.**

In God's picture of atonement in Moses' Law (Lev16), there had to be two goats used: one to die, and one to bear the sins away into the wilderness. In order to fully make atonement for sin, Jesus had to die, rise again, and serve as our High Priest applying His blood to the mercy seat in Heaven for us as we confess our sins and press on walking in the light (1Jo 1:7-9; He 7:25). We must be fully reconciled to God and His Law or we must be executed.

Pardoning the repentant sinner; and satisfying the Law through atonement, rather than the execution of the penalty, seeks a greater good; which is why it is even considered and acceptable. Consider the Apostle Paul: Had God executed the penalty of the Law; Paul's damnation would have served to uphold the Law through retributive justice. Wasn't it a much grander goal to convert, pardon, and enlist him in the service of the Lord to "preach the faith which he once destroyed"? Of course! And BECAUSE Paul repented, surrendered, suffered, and served with all his might, God's choice to pardon, rather than execute was **justified**; and Jesus' atonement in his behalf was also **justified**. However, if Paul had proven to be a Simon, Judas, Demas, etc; it would have undermined God's integrity and credibility if He **saved him anyway**. God's investment of love and mercy in Paul was fully justified, because of his faithfulness. God's mercy on me must be justified daily, or He will withdraw it. God is justified in resisting the proud and giving grace to the humble. God is the master of appropriateness in the administration of His government, which is why Jesus had to die for sinners to be pardoned. God would not justify one sinner unless He could be JUST in doing so.

Consider reading Hebrews 11 if all the men were lazy, faithless, wretches who just prayed a "sinner's prayer" and lived in worldly carnality. What would this say about God's holiness? What would it say about Christ's wisdom in dying and saving them? What message would it send to God's loyal subjects? (Ez. 13:22) It certainly would not make Him JUST and the JUSTIFIER of those that believe in Jesus. You must live in such a way that you justify your justification and vindicate God's salvation plan or you betray your savior and bring reproach upon the Gospel.

Heb 11:16 *But now they desire a better country, that is, an heavenly:* **wherefore God is not ashamed to be called their God:** *for he hath prepared for them a city.*

Mt 7:21 *Not every one that saith unto me, Lord, Lord, shall enter into the kingdom of heaven;* **but he that doeth the will** *of my Father which is in heaven.*

By demanding that we become disciples of Jesus Christ, and suffer for his cause (*Ph. 1:29*), as a true test of our repentance and sincere conversion, God has thoroughly protected against any idea that He sympathizes with sin. He made Jesus the administrator of salvation because He "loved righteousness and hated iniquity" (Heb. 1:8,9); and only those who obey and please Him will be saved (Heb. 5:9).   See: Mark 8:34-38; 2 Cor. 6:17-7:1, etc.

Satan, by his false antinomian Gospel with no demand of repentance, obedience, and faithfulness is trying to misrepresent God, and thereby destroy the influence of God's Law and government – Satan hopes to defeat the effects of the atonement:
- By insinuating that God sympathizes with sinners
- By reducing or diluting the manifestation of God's hatred for sin
- By implying that sinners are victims, rather than deserving of God's wrath

- By implying that God actually created some to be sinners
- And by implying that God doesn't expect us to obey his law – that he never intended us to do so, or that we can't, etc.

Satan, in all this, is striving to slander the holiness and righteousness of God's Law and government – WHY? To cover his own rebellion!

The Antinomian gospel of "easy believe-ism" and "once saved – always saved" is destroying law and order in America as it did it in Israel; because the proper respect and fear of God's Law and government is eroding fast! Jesus had to display a perfect hatred for iniquity (lawlessness), and love for righteousness to even qualify as the Lamb to be slain:

Heb 1:8 *But unto the Son he saith, Thy throne, O God, is for ever and ever: a sceptre of righteousness is the sceptre of thy kingdom. 9* **Thou hast loved righteousness, and hated iniquity; therefore God, even thy God, hath anointed thee with the oil of gladness above thy fellows.**

Jesus had to be extremely important, innocent and pure; and die and suffer sufficient agony, shame, and reproach, to display God's hatred of our sin, the importance of the Law, His determination to uphold the righteousness of his Law, and His unwillingness to compromise or sympathize with sin or sinners.

All of this! So my pardon would not compromise God and harm His government! All of this just to keep me from burning in hell under the righteous wrath of God! Amazing Grace!

For God to forgive us and just allow us to go on violating His Law would destroy his credibility as a just ruler. Putting Jesus' righteousness on our record (as some teach) and allowing us to live unrighteous would also destroy his credibility. Jesus' righteousness is on His own record. His cleansing blood is washing mine as I strive to fulfill His Law by walking in the Light! (I John 1:7-9)

God's way of doing things is due to Him considering all the angles and every legal principle. His way is the only way that doesn't produce bad side effects. God's righteousness is always appropriate. Satan's false clinics may promise an even more "amazing grace", but it will turn out to be an illegal and unsustainable arrangement. Satan's false gospel and false spirituality may sound real special; but it is a lie. If it sounds "holy", but is contrary to the clear word of God, it is false piety. It may appear more holy, but in reality it is not holy at all. We must never trust our heart; but must listen and embrace what God's Word actually says or we will be deceived.

"Which things have indeed a shew of wisdom in will worship, and humility, and neglecting of the body; not in any honour to the satisfying of the flesh." Col. 2:23

Chapter Eleven

Some Lies and False Piety of the Devil's Clinics

False piety is the most subtle way Satan confuses the issues of salvation and thus tries to make good look evil and evil look good. Listen to what the Bible says will happen when people believe Satan's false piety:

2Pe 2:2 *And many shall follow their pernicious ways;* **by reason of whom the way of truth shall be evil spoken of. (2 Cor 11:1-4,13,14)**

This is how it works: Satan perverts the Gospel with false preachers offering an unrealistic "grace" that panders to the feelings of carnal men who sympathize with sin and carnal values. This false grace and false love that Satan knows is unrealistic, illegal, and actually slanders God's righteousness is wrapped up in a false gospel with a false concept of Jesus. It has Jesus delivering us from the "unfair" demands of God's "too strict" law; and giving us liberty to do as we please. It makes us the victims of sin, rather than the villains who must repent of our enmity toward God's authority. It relieves us from obeying God's "unrealistic" moral laws and lets us just do what we deem "loving". God allowing us to do what we think best without demanding we obey his laws is what they call "grace".

This false Gospel has Jesus obeying God in my place so I don't have to; and has God sympathizing with my rebellion because the law was just too hard. Ultimately it has Jesus dying to deliver us from God's failed "plan A", and to give us "plan B"; which is all "love and grace", instead of "Law and obedience". This false Gospel is derived by Satan who is eternally trying to blame God for his own rebellion and failure. Satan trying to put the blame on God is where Calvinistic predestination actually came from long before Calvin was born.

By promising heaven with no heaven to give, Satan distracts men from the true strait and narrow way that leads to genuine salvation and eternal life. If you are thankful for medicine that will save your life, but tastes like bitter herb tea; will you not be *even happier* with medicine that claims it can save your life, yet tastes like soda-pop? What if this is unrealistic and only the bitter herb tea can really save you? When the false prophet speaks of unconditional love and grace to those who have not repented, the true prophet steps up and declares that without repentance, these people are not yet eligible for grace and mercy; but are still in grave danger. Immediately this true prophet is labeled as an unloving and ungracious bigot who doesn't understand our *loving* Heavenly Father. Thus the wicked are justified and promised heaven, while the righteous are vilified as unloving Pharisees who don't know God. This controversy is not new.

Eze 13:22 Because with lies ye have made the heart of the righteous sad, whom I have not made sad; and **strengthened the hands of the wicked**, that he should not return from his wicked way, **by promising him life:**

Isa 5:20 *Woe unto them that call evil good, and good evil; that put darkness for light, and light for darkness; that put bitter for sweet, and sweet for bitter! 21 Woe unto them that are wise in their own eyes, and prudent in their own sight! 23* **Which justify the wicked for reward, and take away the righteousness of the righteous from him!**

Jude 11 *Woe unto them! for they have gone in the way of Cain, and ran greedily after the error of Balaam* **for reward***, and perished in the gainsaying of Core.... **16** These are murmurers, complainers, walking after their own lusts; and their mouth speaketh great swelling words,* **having men's persons in admiration because of advantage.**

I Jn 2:3 *And hereby we do know that we know him, if we keep his commandments. 4* **He that saith, I know him, and keepeth not his commandments, is a liar, and the truth is not in him.** *5 But whoso keepeth his word, in him verily is the love of God perfected: hereby know we that we are in him. 6 He that saith he abideth in him ought himself also so to walk, even as he walked.*

False faith trusting in a false gospel is a poisoned candy that tastes really good to candy lovers; but leads them to eternal death. We have a real enemy who is very powerful and shrewd. He is studying you in order to plan your fall. You cannot afford to be lazy, gullible, naive, careless, or confident in your own ability, strength, and wisdom.

Eph 6:10 *Finally, my brethren, be strong in the Lord, and in the power of his might. 11 Put on the whole armour of God, that ye may be able to stand against the wiles of the devil. 12 For we wrestle not against flesh and blood, but against principalities, against powers, against the rulers of the darkness of this world, against spiritual wickedness in high places. 13 Wherefore take* *unto you the whole armour of God, that ye may be able to withstand in the evil day, and having done all, to stand. 14 Stand therefore, having your loins girt about with truth, and having on the breastplate of righteousness; 15 And your feet shod with the preparation of the gospel of peace; 16 Above all, taking the shield of faith, wherewith ye shall be able to quench all the fiery darts of the wicked. 17 And take the helmet of salvation, and the sword of the Spirit, which is the word of God: 18 Praying always with all prayer and supplication in the Spirit, and watching thereunto with all perseverance and supplication for all saints;*

God offers spiritual armor and weaponry which in a very real way can save your life, your soul, and those you lead or protect (1Ti 4:16). Don't ever assume Satan will only appear in a red suit with a pointed tail and a pitch fork. He will most likely appear as an angel of light, i.e. a very religious and "spiritual" disguise (2Co 11:14). Satan's ministers will be often some of the nicest, most pleasant people you will meet. They will speak well, but not live according to God's Word (2Co 11:15). Even if I preach right; but live wrong; what am I really promoting? I am telling you that believing a right creed while not living holy and humble in obedience to God's Word will still save you – IT WON'T! I've heard many preachers say GOOD THINGS; but their life, family, church order, and example in general are not a display of humble obedience to God's Word. If they are not obeying, then they are teaching you that you can be safe before God while in disobedience – *"Ye shall not surely die."*

The armor of God has everything to do with loving God's righteousness and truth above all. All the armor mentioned will directly or indirectly protect your mind and heart; as it is all about righteousness, truth, right doctrine, faith, and a proper hope. Loving and appreciating God's righteousness is paramount to your spiritual survival. Lovers of righteousness will be the ones who work their way out of the mire of error and deception to find the narrow path that leads to life. If you are just seeking power, prestige, and a promised heavenly abode; then you are not even born again; but still in deception. Once you repent and enlist in Christ's service, then you have power to overcome. Satan cannot destroy you against your will. You are the only one that can give Satan the victory over you. This book is simply sharing some of what I have learned concerning truth and error to help you win if you choose to.

Let's consider some false piety and common lies of Satan's false clinics. False piety is a false concept dressed up to appear more spiritual and exciting than even the truth itself. If we refuse to trust our human feelings and insist on listening to what God's Word actually says on the subject, then we will be delivered from the deception of false piety.

1. "Justified by God's grace means I stand "just-if-I'd" never sinned, i.e. "just as if I'd never sinned"

Sounds pretty, but it is not true. This is a lie – you are seen and stand as a pardoned criminal, not justified as though you never sinned or were the one who was right after all. You are a guilty criminal that has been pardoned, washed, and are under testing and training. Like it or not, you are on probation as your faith and loyalty are being tested to know the genuineness of your repentance and faith. Jesus is your High Priest/probation-officer who administrates the program for your rehabilitation/ sanctification.

2. **"If I comply with standards of holiness and separation from worldliness because I'm commanded to and not because I desire to, I'm living under the Law and not grace."**

The grace of God teaches us that denying ungodliness and worldly lusts, we should live soberly, righteously and godly in this present world. If you do what God says because He commands it, then it means you fear God and believe Him. If there is a conflict with what you **desire**, then you need to repent and stop being a hypocrite, because God will expose this conflict in time. You cannot fool God, so get your desire in line with truth. If God ordained authority is giving you God's Word, then you need to submit, not claim to wait for "God to speak to you" – He already has through His chosen channel.

3. **"We need to focus more on how big and wonderful God is, and avoid the negative preaching about sin and hell."**

By focusing on how incredibly big and gracious and loving God is; and then on how small we are in comparison; people feel better in their sin. If God is so big, and I am so small, then surely He doesn't expect much out of me; and to Him my sin must be really small just like me. Modern ear ticklers follow this format of preaching God's unconditional love; God's total control of everything (Calvinistic Sovereignty); and God's incomprehensible forgiveness to everyone. This is that subtle false piety where Satan offers something unrealistic and illegal to make truth appear less glorious. If you have been fed soda-pop for too long, you will not appreciate the wonderful taste of fresh apple cider or grape juice; even though they are far superior in every way. God's greatness means He knows my very thoughts and will judge just like His Word declares.

4. "If I have to obey God, and this affects my ultimate salvation, then salvation is by works and not by faith and grace."

I think we have sufficiently answered this in previous chapters; but it is indeed a lie of the devil's false clinics to confuse people about their need to meet the covenant conditions. If you cannot provide your own spaghetti, then you ought to be glad to eat what God has placed before you in just the way He has told you to eat it. If you cannot provide your own cure, then be happy to follow the strict orders of the Great Physician.

In today's deceptive false gospel people are more concerned about when you "got saved" and if you really "got it", than if you are actually following and obeying Jesus. If someone turned from their sinful life and started following the teachings of Jesus, praying to Him, and aligning their life with His Word and example; people would be very concerned that they were not trying to be saved by "works", and would want to know if they had first "accepted Christ" or were "trusting Christ completely" for their salvation. They would not think that this man's following and obeying Christ as his Lord and King counted for "trusting Christ". Why? Because they think the essence of salvation is simply trusting Christ's sacrifice on the cross as their substitute and atonement so they are forgiven and have a righteous standing with God without having to actually live righteous. They should be trusting Christ himself as their Lord, King, shepherd and Savior so they actually obey and follow Him. Trusting what Christ did for us AND trusting His prescription for life are both necessary, but to say you are trusting Christ's sacrifice as your substitute without actually trusting Him as your Lord, King, Guide, Master, etc. will leave you without Salvation. Why? Because Jesus only applies His atonement to those who are under His Lordship and thus striving to obey all His teachings. So only the ones who have repented of going their own way, and are now striving to live righteous before God, will be also counted righteous based on Christ's sacrifice. Let me be more clear: You will not be counted righteous unless you are actually striving to live righteous. Those simply "presuming" they will be covered by Christ's blood because they prayed a prayer and told God they were trusting Jesus to save them will be sadly surprised that God expected them to OBEY Jesus to SHOW they were trusting Him to save them. Jesus came to not only save you from hell, but primarily to save you from your sin and self. Jesus expected to save you from hell BY saving you from your sinful way and leading you into a new narrow path that leads to life. His atonement was never meant to save you from hell without first saving you from your sinful selfish way.

5. **"If I submit to the covenant conditions or clinic training before I really want to or feel convicted that I need to – then I am following man and not being led by the Spirit."**

How silly this idea is in light of the fact that God set up the church to perfect the saints. We are to obey the church leaders unless they command us to disobey God. When it is clear that our spiritual leaders are commanding us to go contrary to God's plain Word, then we obey God rather than men (Heb 13:17). Many people are deceived into thinking that being led of the Spirit means "I feel like it",

"I desire it", etc.; but this is deception. They are actually desiring to follow their APPETITE, and then claim to be "led by the Spirit". The apostle Paul said of these people, "Their god is their belly", which reveals that they were just following their appetite while claiming to be led of God. Obeying God and being led of His Spirit is simply obeying the Bible and submitting to God's program in a Biblical church. If you are not doing this, then you are just following your belly.

6. **"If somebody makes me feel guilty for not obeying the King's decrees, they are then bringing me into bondage, when if I just follow the Spirit and do what I feel like doing, I'm walking in liberty."**

Here is another sly cover for an unconverted heart hiding in the "profession of Christianity" while still in bondage to iniquity. Gospel Liberty is freedom from sin's bondage and the corresponding condemnation of God's law. It is liberty from the debt we owe due to our trespasses; but not liberty to continue in trespasses. It is not freedom to do as I please without submitting to God ordained authority. If I am being led of the Spirit according to God's Word, then no person can make me feel guilty for not obeying God; because I **will be** obeying God. The Holy Spirit never led anyone contrary to God's Word. If you see selfishness and sin as drowning in destruction, then you will understand Christian Liberty as walking free of the mire on the narrow road that leads to eternal life in holiness and righteousness. Liberty has everything to do with "where you want to be"; because what one calls bondage is liberty to another. If I want to be inside God's fence, then that to me is liberty. If I want to be outside God's fence, then being inside is bondage to me.

7. "If I obey the King's conditions and strive to please Him in every way, then somehow I'm offending Him and frustrating His grace, because I'm trying to help pay for my redemption, rather than just believing in Jesus."

If one was actually foolish enough to think that they were paying for their salvation by obeying the doctor, then it would be offensive, but I really don't think anyone is that stupid. This is simply a false accusation by those who don't want to obey God and live holy which they fling upon others who are making them look bad. In our parables and previous discussion we've already answered this false piety that claims to be pleasing God more by doing nothing than by obeying.

8. "If I do something because the church, preacher, and Bible tell me to, but it is not from my heart, then I shouldn't do it."

You should always do what is right whether told to or not; and if your heart is in the way, then repent and ask God to clean up your wicked heart.

9. "Striving to be a good trainee, learn fast, study hard, live vigilant, honor the King, wear my badge in plain sight – If I think this makes me more in the King's favor and gives me a better chance of being accepted in the end, I'm deceived and am really no better off than those who just stick the badge in their pocket, because we will all be accepted by grace, and all our efforts to please the king are seen as filthy rags which only reveal that we are proud

and think we can actually do anything that pleases the king."

This lie of the devil is based on false concepts about salvation by grace, as though grace puts everyone on the same plain. Why then did Noah find grace in the eyes of the Lord while everyone else was drowned? If we think of these concepts according to common sense instead of some mystical Calvinistic nonsense, then we can see that any king would have more favor toward a servant who strove to please him than toward a servant who didn't. The Bible **never** says our **righteousness** is filthy rags before God. In Isa 64:6 the prophet declares that all Israel's **religiosity**, **ritual observances** or "**righteousnesses**" while they were not broken, humble, and obedient to God were "filthy rags"; but this is a completely different issue. Isaiah never said their good deeds and striving to please God were filthy rags. Read your Bible and you will see that God is pleased over and over with those who humbly strive to obey His Word. Hundreds of verses testify to this, and only ignorance of the Bible would ever lead someone to say that God sees our faithful obedience and righteousness as filthy rags.

10. "Since our salvation is not by 'works of righteousness that we have done', then there is no necessity of doing works of righteousness."

We have already covered this subtle slippery lie of the serpent. It is the same lie he told Eve, *"If you disobey God, ye shall not surely die"*. Shall we continue in sin that grace may abound? **God forbid!** Shall we continue in sin because we are not under the law, but under grace? **God forbid! Know ye not, that to whom ye yield yourselves**

servants to obey, his servants ye are to whom ye obey; whether of sin unto death, or of obedience unto righteousness? If you yield your members to sin you will get what?? DEATH.

11. **"We can't do anything to gain God's favor; we just have to believe that He loves us and forgives us because of Jesus."**

Is this what the Bible says? The Bible says the Angels rejoice when one sinner repents. Jesus was pleased when he saw the faith of the centurion. God was obviously pleased with Cornelius. The Bible is jam-packed with God showing his displeasure against rebellion and his pleasure toward humble obedience. Just a simple reading of the Bible declares without controversy that God is pleased with humble contrite obedience; but is angry with proud disobedience.

12. **"We shouldn't obey God because we fear Him, but just because we love Him and desire to please Him."**

This is subtle, but not accurate. True love of God never eliminates a proper fear of God. People get this false idea from the verse that says "Perfect love casteth out fear" (1Jn 4:18); but this is not speaking of the fear of the Lord. It is speaking of "dread". If, as a child, I have a healthy fear of my earthly father, knowing that I should not cross him, I am still happy and excited when he comes home if I have been obedient, and love him. The fear of the Lord is the beginning of wisdom, and perfect love doesn't cast out wisdom. Perfect love casts out dread, which is a fear due to my disobedience and guilt – like Adam had after he sinned. Proper love and desire to please God stem from a proper fear and reverence for him – they cannot be properly separated.

13. "If I think that anything I do can affect my salvation, then I'm not trusting Jesus alone to save me."

Who, in our parable was trusting the doctor alone to save them? Was it the ones who were doing everything he said, or the ones doing only part? Did Jesus say, "Come unto me"? If you do that, are you then not trusting Jesus *alone* to save you? Did Jesus say, "Except ye repent, ye shall all likewise perish"? If you repent, are you then not trusting Jesus *alone* to save you? The false piety that says *trusting Jesus alone to save me* is contrary to my diligent obedience to Jesus' commands is sheer stupidity.

14. "God forgives our sins, past, present, and future."

Doesn't this sound sweet? Is it realistic? God never forgives future sins, because they do not exist. There is no condemnation until there is trespass. If you have not trespassed, then you have not sinned (1Jn 3:4). Why would Jesus need to intercede for us and continually cleanse us as our High Priest if sins were forgiven in the future? One Baptist pastor had a lady come up to him after the sermon with her concern, "Pastor, I don't understand how my sins could be forgiven – past, present, and future" He gave her a confident smile and answered, "Ma'm, all your sins were future when Jesus died on the cross". Do you see any problem with his answer? Obviously he didn't, for he printed it in his book! Can you imagine such shallow thinking? Everyone's sins in the last 2000 years were future when Jesus died on the cross, but does that mean they are all forgiven? Do they not need to repent to be saved? Of Course they do.   This unrealistic forgiveness is foolishness.

15. "I'm just trusting in the finished work of Christ on the cross."

This sounds pious, but if you are doing that you will go to hell.   When Jesus said, "It is finished" everything regarding our salvation was not complete, and nobody would be saved if He stopped right there. What if Jesus had not risen? What if Jesus had not placed His own blood on the mercy seat in Heaven? What if Jesus did not become our high priest to minister for us in the tabernacle of Heaven? Jesus' atonement included His Sacrifice AND His Priesthood.   In God's picture of atonement in Lev. 16, God used two goats: one to die, and one to live and be driven away into the wilderness. One pictured Christ's death and the other His resurrected priesthood in the heavens. BOTH were necessary for a full atonement.

What if Jesus did not commission the Apostles and send the Holy Ghost at Pentecost? What if Jesus did not provide us with the New Testament Scriptures? Shall I go on, or are you willing to realize that this false piety is deception of the devil. There is a narrow road you must get on and stay on till you die, or you will go to hell while "trusting the finished work of Christ on the cross". Trust his priesthood and lordship now to the point that you act appropriately.   If you trust your doctor, you take the prescription!

16. "Jesus' righteousness is put on my record, so God only sees His Son, and not me. I am clothed in the

righteousness of Jesus and His righteousness is imputed to me."

Then why does Jesus need to be your High Priest to intercede to the Father and continually cleanse your record?? Jesus' righteousness is NOT on your record; but on Jesus' record. His blood cleanses my record, which declares me righteous by God's grace and Jesus' sacrifice; but God never will see me as righteous as His own beloved Son. In order for Jesus to be the spotless Lamb of God, he had to be sinless before God. His obedience was on **His** record so He could die in my place. His obedience was not vicarious, only His death was. His obedience made him eligible to die for me; but he did not obey for me and then put his works on my record. This is a lie of false piety.

"Jesus is our righteousness" **only** in the sense that His blood cleanses our sin record and His priesthood keeps it clean as we walk in the light and confess known sins (I Jo 1-9; He 7:25). The Bible clearly and undeniably explains the imputation of righteousness to the believer as simply the NON-IMPUTATION OF SINS or the cleansing of his record before God and keeping it clean by the priesthood of Christ. This is a concept known to Abraham before Moses' Law, known to David under the Law, and still relevant for everyone in the New Covenant. It is all the same Gospel Salvation from Genesis to Revelation. Listen to Romans chapter 4 as Paul is explaining this very concept:

Ro 4:5 But to him that worketh not **[for self atonement]***, but believeth on him that justifieth the ungodly, his* **faith is counted for righteousness.** *6 Even as David also* **describeth the blessedness of the man, unto whom God imputeth**

125

*righteousness without works, 7 **Saying,** Blessed are they whose iniquities are forgiven, and whose sins are covered. 8 Blessed is the man to whom the Lord will not impute sin.*

Plain words that cannot be denied: *the imputation of righteousness to the believer is simply the washing of the record – the non-imputation of trespasses.* **We do not have God's or Jesus' personal righteousness imputed to us or our record.** A clean record is what is required by God, which declares that my transgressions are pardoned.

Often when the Bible uses the term "God's righteousness" or "the righteousness of God" it is referring to God's "Justification program", not His *personal* righteousness and therefore people get quite confused not knowing the Scriptures. This confusion is the root of much error and heresy. The word "righteousness" and the word "justification" come from the same Greek word and are often interchangeable because we are talking about being ***declared righteous*** before God on His terms, which is exactly what ***Gospel justification*** is. When the Bible speaks about the "gift of righteousness" it is simply speaking about the "gift of Gospel justification" through Christ's cleansing blood. When we are cleansed by the Blood of the Lamb, we need nothing else. Any other teaching is error. The imputation of righteousness is the NON-IMPUTATION OF SIN due to the Christ's blood cleansing my record.

17. **"Unless we believe that we are unconditionally secure and can't fall out of favor with the King, then we are completely insecure and cannot have a right relationship with the King."**

If you know the conditions of the covenant, then you know when you are in and when you are out. The covenant makes provision for failure or recovery; but not

126

for rebellion. Does any son think the inheritance is unconditionally his apart from having a good relationship with his father? Does he know what exactly it would take to make his father disinherit him? Maybe not; but he does know how to stay in his father's favor, and usually wants to – AS long as the relationship is sweet, there is no insecurity. If He blunders, he should fear and be concerned and work to make it right. While he maintains a good relationship with his father through honor, obedience and productive communication, he is secure that his receiving the inheritance is not in danger.

Any child knows what to do to make Mommy or Daddy happy when they come home; and they also know what to do to make the parents very unhappy when they come home. If the child has done what they know will please the parent, then they are excited when they come home, and are not insecure; but the opposite is also true. Hey, even dogs can figure this out. Have you ever come home to a dog sulking around guilty? I have, and I began wondering what he did wrong. Once we came home and the dog had killed a chicken – boy, did he act guilty. WE KNOW what it would take to make our meeting with Jesus a happy one or an unhappy one. Unconditional security for the believer is a presumptuous and arrogant affront to the clear conditions God has set on the New Covenant. It is a foolish self deception that will end in a deadly reality.

18. "We shouldn't force our children to dress and live right because we want their good deeds to be from their heart."

The Bible commands us to bring up our children in the nurture and admonition of the Lord. The Bible exhorts us to train up our children in the way they should go. Many

127

Scriptures teach that we should not only tell our children what is right, but command, train, correct, chasten, and lead them in what is right. While they live in our home, they should have to live godly and righteous. We pray, "thy kingdom come, thy will be done on earth as it is in heaven"; but do we realize that it is our responsibility to see that His will is done on earth where we have jurisdiction and authority? In our home we must see to it that His will is enforced like it is in heaven. Our children's conversion will solve the issue of it being in their heart. If we don't hold up the standards of righteousness in our home, then we are teaching the children a false concept of God's will. Do we expect they will raise the standard in our home after we let it drop?

19. "God never expected men to obey His Law, because we cannot obey His Laws. God just gave the law to show us we cannot obey it."

Ha! Tell Zacharias and Elisabeth that:

Luke1:6 *And they were both righteous before God, walking in all the commandments and ordinances of the Lord blameless."*

This lie is very popular with Calvinists; but it is still a lie of the Devil's false clinics. Any intelligent person who reads through the entire Bible will see that God expected men to obey His laws; was angry when they didn't; punished them when they didn't; and was pleased when they did. So, you want me to believe you HAVE to lie, steal, kill, commit adultery, dishonor your parents, have other God's, etc.??? Get your head out of the theology book and read your Bible. We know that men cannot present a perfect record of obedience to God, and are under condemnation; but we also know that their condemnation is just because they could have obeyed.

We also know that those who walk in the Spirit fulfill the righteousness of the Law. Do a search on a good Bible study program: punch in "Keep Commandments" and see all the verses where God expects men to keep His commandments. God never commanded men to do what they could not. God would never condemn a man for inability, but only rebellion. Only those who repent and keep his commandments will be saved.

Re 22:14 *Blessed are they that do his commandments, that they may have right to the tree of life, and may enter in through the gates into the city.*

I Jo 2:3 *And hereby we do know that we know him, **if we keep his commandments.** 4 He that saith, I know him, and keepeth not his commandments, is a liar, and the truth is not in him. 5 But **whoso keepeth his word,** in him verily is the love of God perfected: hereby know we that we are in him.*

The Bible says the Law of Moses was our school master to bring us to Christ; and this has been twisted to mean that the Law taught us that we cannot be good and obey God; but must simply trust Christ to save us without us actually striving to obey and live holy. The truth of the matter is that the Law of Moses was a wonderful object lesson about Christ's salvation program.

What our God ordained school master taught us:

a. The Law of Moses was in two parts: the moral plumb line that shows man is crooked and in need of atonement; and then the tabernacle: which taught them about God's salvation through blood atonement, priesthood, etc.

b. The Law taught us that God will not have a relationship with fallen man outside of God's conditional covenant arrangements. If we would reconcile with God, we must come under such a covenant that God has devised.

c. The Law taught that "without the shedding of blood there is no remission of sin". We cannot hope to have a forensic justification based on our perfect record, but must obtain a pardon by God's grace through repentance, obedience, and a blood sacrifice to cover transgression.

d. The Law taught us about priesthood, and how to relate to God through a priest. We need to "come unto God by him" (Heb. 7:25), and keep our record clean before God.

e. The Law taught us about the "Lamb of God" that takes away the sins of the world. It taught that this lamb must be pure and without blemish, etc. God taught man about the "Lamb of God" shedding his blood for the remission of sins for thousands of years before He sent Jesus, **and man, for the most part, still missed it!**

f. The Law taught us about the difference between clean and unclean, holy and unholy; and the need to keep ourselves clean in order to have a relationship with God.

g. The Law taught us that without submission and obedience to the moral laws of God, you are not even eligible for the forgiveness and cleansing of the blood atonement that God has provided. **A Jew who was put out of the assembly or "cut off" from his people through trespass and apostasy gained no benefit from the Day of Atonement, and had no access to God through the priest (Numbers 15)**

h. We are taught the difference between "ignorant sin" and "presumptuous sin". The willful sin spoken of in

Hebrews 10:26 is referring directly to Numbers 15, and what is taught there.

i. Every example in the New Covenant about salvation is from an Old Covenant person or situation. Without the Old Covenant Scriptures we cannot fully understand or appreciate the New Covenant!

In the New Covenant, we have Christ as our High Priest in the Tabernacle of Heaven offering His own blood for our sins. We must still follow many principles taught in the Old Covenant so we can properly relate to our High Priest, and appreciate what He is doing for us. Most people don't understand the mechanics (how it works) of salvation; and this causes much confusion to Satan's delight. If they would study to understand the Old Covenant mechanics of salvation, it would teach them the New Covenant mechanics of salvation.

*I Jn 1:5 ¶ This then is the message which we have heard of him, and declare unto you, that God is light, and in him is no darkness at all. 6 If we say that we have fellowship with him, and walk in darkness, we lie, and do not the truth: 7 But __if we walk in the light, as he is in the light__, we have fellowship one with another, __and the blood of Jesus Christ his Son cleanseth us from all sin.__ 8 ¶ If we say that we have no sin, we deceive ourselves, and the truth is not in us. 9 **If** we confess our sins, he is faithful and just to forgive us our sins, and to cleanse us from all unrighteousness.*

This is just what the school master taught us: We must walk in the light God gives or we have no fellowship and are not eligible for the benefits of the atonement. If we walk in the light of God's holy moral laws, then we can have a relationship with God, and we are then eligible for the benefits of Christ as our High Priest. While we walk in the light, doing what we know to be right in God's sight; our High Priest keeps our record clean. If we know we have sinned, we must come to our High Priest (Jesus) and confess our sins for cleansing and forgiveness.

Perpetual justification is dependent upon perpetual walking in the light (faith). We are justified by faith: that means as long as faith keeps walking in the light, we continue to be justified through Christ's priestly service. A "faith" that stops walking in the light is no longer faith, but unbelief; and when this happens, our justification stops, because Christ stops cleansing our record until we repent and start walking in the light again. Walking in the light is synonymous with "walking in the Spirit", "having the obedience of faith", "walking on the narrow way", or, "living by faith" – they all mean the same thing.

While we are walking in the light, we will have two types of sins: known trespass and unknown trespass. The known trespasses must be confessed and repented of, or they become willful rebellion and we have *"no more sacrifice for sin, but a certain looking for of judgment and fiery indignation" (Heb. 10:26).* If we confess our sins, Jesus, our High Priest will cleanse us and our record in heaven. The ignorant sins are automatically covered while we are walking faithfully in the light we have and willing to receive and obey more.

Heb 7:22 *By so much was Jesus made a surety of a better Covenant. 23 And they truly were many priests, because they were not suffered to continue by reason of death: 24 But this man, because he continueth ever, hath an unchangeable priesthood.*

132

25 Wherefore he is able also to save them to the uttermost that come unto God by him, seeing he ever liveth to make intercession for them.

Here we see that Jesus is a much greater High Priest; but we must continually come and make use of His services <u>so we can be saved all the way to the end</u>. The word "come" in verse 25 is "present participle" in the Greek and means to "keep coming". If we don't keep coming to our High Priest and making confession, He will not keep interceding and "keeping us saved" to the uttermost – to the end. The schoolmaster has taught us all these principles; and we must follow them in order to be saved by the Faith of Christ.

20. "If you strive to live holy, separated unto God, and are careful to obey all the Bible teaches; and then you expect others to do the same, you are a Pharisee, or just the *weaker brother*."

Yes, this is just another front for carnal rebellious men to hide behind. The Pharisees were not faulted for obeying God too much; but for not obeying Him enough. They were hypocrites who put on a front of holiness, but were covetous and selfish in their hearts. They were doing what produced the best results in worldly gain. Usually those who call obedient believers Pharisees are truly Pharisees themselves in that **they are doing what brings the best results in worldly gain rather than sincerely obeying God at any cost.** Pharisees who sincerely obeyed God's law would not have been rebuked by Jesus. **Read Matthew 23. Jesus taught people to live holy and separated unto God with all their hearts; and then commanded them to preach that others must repent to** be saved. Was Jesus producing Pharisees? Is the Great Commission a plan to produce Pharisees?

Mt 28:19 *Go ye therefore, and teach all nations, baptizing them in the name of the Father, and of the Son, and of the Holy Ghost:*
20 <u>Teaching them to observe all things whatsoever I have commanded you:</u>

On the issue of the "weaker brother" as taken from Romans 14: That chapter is dealing with the relationship of Jews and Gentiles in the same Christian congregation, and is only speaking of such amoral issues as meat, drink, holy days, and such; where both parties on either side of the issue can be righteous and holy before God. The verse just before this chapter commands all of us, "*Ro 13:14 But put ye on the Lord Jesus Christ, and make not provision for the flesh, to fulfil the lusts thereof*"; so absolutely NOTHING in chapter fourteen can be used to excuse carnality or make provision for the flesh to fulfill its lusts. "Righteousness, peace, and joy in the Holy Ghost" are said to be essential for every believer! Last, but certainly not least is the fact that these epistles were written to church leaders, and the applications of these principles were not left to each man to do with what he willed. It was all done within an orderly program under accountability; and mature godly leaders were to decide for the church what issues were indeed amoral and unnecessary.

21. **"Repentance is simply meant to be turning from unbelief, not a turning from sin, because nobody can actually turn from sin."**

Here is a good cover for pastors who claim great soul-winning results; but cannot seem to disciple them. I speak from first hand experience in all these areas, because I was raised in the Baptist church, went to their colleges, and was a Baptist pastor. Repentance in the Bible is a turning from sin in the mind, heart, and life. It is a submission to the God we were at enmity with. The Bible is jammed with verses and scenarios that demonstrate the reality and necessity of repentance from the broad road of sin to the narrow road of obedience. Paul preached that men should repent, and turn to God, and do works meet for repentance. Eternal Security fans are continually trying to get away from the need to obey, because this throws a wrench in their idea that salvation is a "done deal" at the point of conversion. If we must obey, then it is not a "done deal". One famous Baptist pastor who strongly advocated "eternal security" teaching said in my hearing, "If one must repent of sins to be saved, then if he goes back to sins, he will no longer be saved" -- DUH! Of course this is true; but from this he determined repentance could not be from sin, but just unbelief. This doesn't fix his problem, though, because then if someone goes back to unbelief, they still will not be saved. Try as they will, they cannot escape from the common sense truth of God. Some say they believe in repentance and eternal security. Imagine me telling my sons, "You must take your muddy boots off to come in the house; but if you put them back on once in the house, it is alright". That is the logic of saying you believe in repentance and also this "once saved, always saved" heresy.

22. "My outside doesn't matter, because God sees my heart, and so it only matters what is on my inside. If

my heart feels good, then my outward disobedience doesn't matter."

Thousands are hiding behind the false piety that somehow because I think my heart is full of love that my outward disobedience is nullified. They think they have a special relationship with God that exempts them from obeying what the Bible says for everyone else to obey. This is a deep rooted deception, and the following verses will show it is all too common.

*Ps 50:16 But unto the wicked God saith, What hast thou to do to declare my statutes, or that thou shouldest take my covenant in thy mouth? 17 Seeing thou hatest instruction, and castest my words behind thee...21 These things hast thou done, and I kept silence; **thou thoughtest that I was altogether such an one as thyself: but I will reprove thee, and set them in order before thine eyes.***

*I Jn 2:3 And hereby we do know that we know him, if we keep his commandments. 4 **He that saith, I know him, and keepeth not his commandments, is a liar, and the truth is not in him.***

*Jn 14:21 **He that hath my commandments, and keepeth them, he it is that loveth me:** and he that loveth me shall be loved of my Father, and I will love him, and will manifest myself to him...23 Jesus answered and said unto him, **If a man love me, he will keep my words:** and my Father will love him, and we will come unto him, and make our abode with him. 24 **He that loveth me not keepeth not my sayings:***

Jesus said the foolish man who built his house upon the sand was the man who heard His sayings, but did them not. It was of this class of men who said, Lord, Lord, but didn't do the will of His Father. It was this deceived group whose Judgment Day experience is mentioned below.

Mt 7:22 Many will say to me in that day, Lord, Lord, have we not prophesied in thy name? and in thy name have cast out devils? and in thy name done many wonderful works? 23 And then will I profess unto them, I never knew you: depart from me, ye that work iniquity.

Working iniquity means they disregarded God's Laws. The doctrine of the false clinics said they could; but God judges our heart by what we say and do. Jesus said, "Out of the abundance of the heart the mouth speaketh"; thus God knows that your actions and words come from the choices and attitudes of your heart.

23. "As long as I love the Lord and try to be good to people, I will be OK on judgment day"

If you were the King, and you had gone to great pains to provide a program for the rehabilitation and redemption of fallen men so they could again be citizens in your kingdom; how would you feel if they took this attitude of setting their own standards and criteria? Rather than studying and obeying the path you had laid out, they assume their own standards and ideas are sufficient. Is this not a prideful stinking presumption that will also determine how they would obey you once they were in your kingdom? Could this attitude be tolerated in your kingdom? What if all your faithful subjects adopted this attitude of doing as they pleased and expecting you to accept it? This is exactly what Cain did. Cain offered unto God what he wanted to offer – what he thought was good enough; and he expected God to accept it and be pleased. Did He? Was God satisfied with Cain following his own brain and expecting Him to be pleased? Cain also claimed to "love" the Lord, just look at his nice gift. But what does God think about such "love"? Jesus clearly said in **Jn 14:23** *"...If a man love me, he will keep my words: and my Father will love him, and we will come unto him, and make our abode with him.24 He that loveth me not keepeth not my sayings: and the word which ye hear is not mine, but the Father's which sent me."*

24. "As long as I have a relationship with God, I don't have to be a part of a Biblical church body to be pleasing to God"

Read Jn 14:23-24 again. What kind of relationship do you have with God when you don't value HIS program for your sanctification and rehabilitation as preparation for living in His Kingdom? The apostles would not accept your profession of faith as valid without you striving to be a part of a local body of Scriptural believers. In the days of the apostles if you forsook the assembly of the saints, you were committing sin against the Lord (Heb 10:25,26). The church is the bride of Christ, but this is not speaking of some invisible universal body of every scattered believer around the world without biblical structure. It is speaking of local assemblies of believers who are striving to operate according to the apostolic pattern laid out in the Scriptures.

In the days of the apostles, if you were an upstanding member of a church in one city, and you moved to another city where they didn't know you already, the sending church would write for you a letter of commendation, so the church where you were moving could receive you into communion (2Co 3:1). This is how important membership and accountability was to the apostolic churches. Those who rail against church membership as some modern invention simply don't know their Bibles. It was a privilege to be in communion with the local body of Christ. This privilege has responsibilities, and if you don't live up to the faith, you should lose this privilege and be ex-communicated i.e. lose your membership. Your relationship with the church is to be a commitment similar to marriage. The only thing that should cause division is sin; and repentance should mend that division. This means that division with the church is division with Christ unless the church has apostatized rather than you. If you don't value the king's clinics and clinic training, you are simply telling the king that you are still a rebel at heart wanting to be your own king. Don't be surprised when the following scenario is replayed at your judgment.

Mt 7:21 *Not every one that saith unto me, Lord, Lord, shall enter into the kingdom of heaven;* **but he that doeth the will of my Father which is in heaven**. *22 Many will say to me in that day, Lord, Lord, have we not prophesied in thy name? and in thy name have cast out devils? and in thy name done many wonderful works? 23 And then will I profess unto them, I never knew you: depart from me, ye that* **work iniquity (lawlessness)**. *24 Therefore whosoever heareth these sayings of mine, and* **doeth them,** *I will liken him unto a wise man, which built his house upon a rock: 25 And the rain descended, and the floods came, and the winds blew, and beat upon that house; and it fell not: for it was founded upon a rock. 26 And every one that heareth these sayings of mine, and* **doeth them not**, *shall be likened unto a foolish man, which built his house upon the sand: 27 And the rain descended, and the floods came, and the winds blew, and beat upon that house; and it fell: and great was the fall of it.*

25. "Being sincere in your faith is all that matters"

If being sincere in your faith is all that matters for salvation...

- ...Then any faith is as good as another (Catholic, Mormon, JW, Marcionite, Muslim, Hindu, Essene, Jew, etc.), and will work?
- ... Then contending for the faith once delivered to the saints (Jude 3) is a waste of time, and actually militates against the salvation of souls?
- ...Then Paul's concern over a false Jesus, a false Gospel, and a false spirit (2 Cor. 11) was completely unfounded and reveals a lack of understanding?
- ...Then deception is nothing to fear or combat; only insincerity is wrong? (Romans 16:18)
- ...Then false prophets "alluring through the lust of the flesh", and "many following their pernicious ways", is of no concern? (2 Peter 2).
- ...Then the easiest and most popular gospel message is the best, whether true to God's Word or not? (Gal. 1:8,9)
- ...Then the greatest liar, so long as he draws the largest crowd and thoroughly deceives them with his false gospel, is actually the greatest evangelist? (John 8:44)
  - *Mt 15:14 Let them alone: they be blind leaders of the blind. And if the blind lead the blind, __both__ shall fall into the ditch.*
- ...Then I should go preach whatever lie draws the largest crowd of sincere followers? Though I know it to be a lie, as long as I sincerely believe that the end justifies the means, then I will also be saved? (Matt. 7:14; 24:4-11)

...No, No, Sorry, but sincerity of faith alone is not going to save anyone. You must be following the

right Jesus as Lord of your life, and striving to learn and observe all His teachings (Matt. 28:20), or the following may happen to you:

Matt. 7:21 Not every one that saith unto me, Lord, Lord, shall enter into the kingdom of heaven; but he that doeth the will of my Father which is in heaven. 22 Many will say to me in that day, Lord, Lord, have we not prophesied in thy name? and in thy name have cast out devils? and in thy name done many wonderful works? 23 And then will I profess unto them, I never knew you: depart from me, ye that work iniquity.

Notice that "you accepting Christ" is not the final goal; but rather "Christ accepting YOU". Listen to the Lord's conclusion:

Matt. 7:24 Therefore whosoever <u>heareth these sayings of mine, and doeth them</u>, I will liken him unto a wise man, which built his house upon a rock: 25 And the rain descended, and the floods came, and the winds blew, and beat upon that house; and it fell not: for it was founded upon a rock. 26 And every one that <u>heareth these sayings of mine, and doeth them not</u>, shall be likened unto a foolish man, which built his house upon the sand: 27 And the rain descended, and the floods came, and the winds blew, and beat upon that house; and it fell: and great was the fall of it.

*Lu 6:39 And he spake a parable unto them, Can the blind lead the blind? <u>**shall they not both fall into the ditch?**</u>*

Sincerity will not save you unless you are striving to obey all the Word of God you have. Doctrinal inerrancy is not a prerequisite for salvation; but just being sincere and deceived doesn't save either. We don't know how strict or lenient God is going to be on judgment day. We do know that the way is narrow,

141

and *few there be that find it*. We are exhorted in Scripture to pass the time of our sojourning here is fear; and work out our own salvation with fear and trembling.

I Peter 1:15 But as he which hath called you is holy, so be ye holy in all manner of conversation; 16 Because it is written, Be ye holy; for I am holy. 17 And if ye call on the Father, who without respect of persons judgeth according to every man's work, pass the time of your sojourning here in fear:

We do know that ignorance of the Law is no excuse: Romans 1&2 & Luke 12:46

Luke 12:46 The lord of that servant will come in a day when he looketh not for him, and at an hour when he is not aware, and will cut him in sunder, and will appoint him his **portion with the unbelievers.** *47 And that servant, which* **knew his lord's will, and prepared not himself***, neither did according to his will, shall be beaten with many stripes. 48 But he that* **knew not***, and did commit things worthy of stripes, shall be beaten with few stripes. For unto whomsoever much is given, of him shall be much required: and to whom men have committed much, of him they will ask the more.*

There is no room for presumption or carelessness!

Chapter Twelve

The Gospel Of The Kingdom

When Jesus and the apostles went about preaching the glad tidings of the Kingdom of God, what was it they were preaching? What does the Bible teach? Is the church now THE Kingdom or just a foretaste and time of preparation for it? What is it that the believer has to look forward to? What is our hope? What should we expect?

> *Lu 19:11 And as they heard these things, he added and spake a parable, because he was nigh to Jerusalem, and **because they thought that the kingdom of God should immediately appear.** 12 He said therefore, A certain nobleman **went into a far country to receive for himself a kingdom, and to return.** 13 And he called his ten servants, and delivered them ten pounds, and said unto them, **Occupy till I come. 14 But his citizens hated him, and sent a message after him, saying, We will not have this man to reign over us. 15 And it came to pass, that when he was returned, having received the kingdom,** then he commanded these servants to be called unto him, to whom he had given the money, that he might know how much every man had gained by trading. 16 Then came the first, saying, Lord, thy pound hath gained ten pounds. 17 And he said unto him, **Well, thou good servant: because thou hast been faithful in a very little, have thou authority over ten cities.** 18 And the second came, saying, Lord,*

143

*thy pound hath gained five pounds. 19 And he said likewise to him, **Be thou also over five cities** 20 And another came, saying, Lord, behold, here is thy pound, which I have kept laid up in a napkin: 21 For I feared thee, because thou art an austere man: thou takest up that thou layedst not down, and reapest that thou didst not sow. 22 And he saith unto him, Out of thine own mouth will I judge thee, thou wicked servant. Thou knewest that I was an austere man, taking up that I laid not down, and reaping that I did not sow: 23 Wherefore then gavest not thou my money into the bank, that at my coming I might have required mine own with usury? 24 And he said unto them that stood by, Take from him the pound, and give it to him that hath ten pounds. 25 (And they said unto him, Lord, he hath ten pounds.) 26 For I say unto you, That unto every one which hath shall be given; and from him that hath not, even that he hath shall be taken away from him. **27 But those mine enemies, which would not that I should reign over them, bring hither, and slay them before me.***

I try not to be too dogmatic on my interpretations or conclusions concerning "end-time" prophecies; but it seems that many Scriptures cannot be fulfilled without Jesus returning to reign with His saints on planet earth over mortal unregenerate nations (Rev 20, Zech 14). How will we who are saved reign with Christ (Rev 5:10)? Over whom will we reign? Why would Jesus rule the nations with a rod of iron, if they were all converted people (Ps 2:9; Re 2:27; Re 12:5; Re 19:15)? In Revelation 2:27 it says we who overcome in this life will also reign with a rod of iron over the nations and consequently "as the vessels of a potter shall they be broken to shivers:" – the meaning is all too clear, is it not? Who is it that will carry out the command of Jesus upon His return: **"But those mine enemies, which would**

not that I should reign over them, bring hither, and slay them before me."? Who is it that will do this?? It can only be His faithful servants – hopefully that will be you and I! Some may recoil at this; but that only means you have a problem with Jesus. Sorry, He is not a pacifist, and you having a problem with His ways will not set well with him. Do you think you are more holy that Jesus?

We don't know how this Kingdom will occur exactly; but we do know a few things about it. Just looking at this parable we can see that the Kingdom of God was not to immediately appear; that Jesus would be gone for a good while to receive for himself a kingdom and return; that his servants were to be occupied doing his business while he was gone; and that when he returned, having received the kingdom, he would both reward his faithful servants and judge those who opposed him or were unfaithful. We, the Christian Church, are in the category of "occupying" till he comes. He is coming to reign; and his faithful servants will reign with Him over "cities" of people. Who exactly will they be? Will it be on this earth? Will believers be immortal, while those over whom they reign are still mortal? We can be confident on some points; but cannot be dogmatic on all the details. Below are some observations about Christ's Kingdom that are quite certain:

#1 It is not here now in the sense that we are to expect it in the future. Those servants who were commanded to "occupy", were they already in the kingdom? Yes and No. They were already under their king and serving him; but not yet in the kingdom that was coming. The disciples were with Jesus when he told the Pharisees, "The Kingdom of God is within you" and they knew what that meant; but they still asked Jesus in Acts 1:6, "Wilt thou at this time restore again the kingdom to Israel?" We are now to be waiting for a coming kingdom, striving to be worthy to inherit it, and being tested to see if we are faithful in little so we can then be trusted with much (five or ten cities, etc.). As we put Jesus on the throne of our hearts and uphold his Lordship in our lives and the areas where we have jurisdiction or exercise authority, we are experiencing His Kingdom within our lives; but only in a limited sense. Notice in the following Scriptures the difference between what is NOW and what is to be LATER when Jesus returns. I will insert and N for NOW, and a L for LATER.

- **Mt 5:5** *Blessed are the meek (N): for they* **shall inherit** *the earth. (L)*
- **Mt 5:10** *Blessed are they which are persecuted for righteousness' sake (N): for theirs is the kingdom of heaven. (L)*
- **Mt 5:19** *Whosoever therefore shall break one of these least commandments, and shall teach men so (N), he* **shall be** *called the least in the kingdom of heaven (L): but whosoever shall do and teach them (N), the same* **shall be** *called great in the kingdom of heaven. (L)*
- **Mt 5:20** *For I say unto you, That except your righteousness shall exceed the righteousness of the scribes and Pharisees (N), ye shall in no case enter into the kingdom of heaven.(L)*
- **Mt 6:10** *Thy kingdom come. Thy will be done in earth, as it is in heaven.*
- **Mt 7:21** *¶Not every one that saith unto me, Lord, Lord, (N) shall enter into the kingdom of heaven (L); but he that doeth the will of my Father which is in heaven. (N).*
- **Mt 25:34 Then** *shall the King say unto them on his right hand, Come, ye blessed of my Father,* **inherit the**

kingdom prepared for you from the foundation of the world:

- **Ac 1:6** *When they therefore were come together, they asked of him, saying, Lord, wilt thou at this time restore again the kingdom to Israel?*
- **Ac 3:21** *Whom the heaven must receive **until the times of restitution of all things**, which God hath spoken by the mouth of all his holy prophets since the world began.*
  - This time of restitution relates to "the regeneration" spoken of in Mt 19:27 below in #2
- **Ac 14:22** *Confirming the souls of the disciples, and exhorting them to continue in the faith, and that **we must through much tribulation (N) enter into the kingdom of God. (L)***
- **1Co 6:9** ¶ *Know ye not that the unrighteous (N) shall not inherit the kingdom of God?(L)*
- **2Th 1:5** *Which is a manifest token of the righteous judgment of God, **that ye may be counted worthy of the kingdom of God,(L) for which ye also suffer (N)***
- **2Ti 4:1** ¶ *I charge thee therefore before God, and the Lord Jesus Christ, who shall judge the quick and the dead **at his appearing and his kingdom;***
- **2Ti 4:18** *And the Lord shall deliver me from every evil work, and will **preserve me unto his heavenly kingdom**: to whom be glory for ever and ever. Amen.*
- **Heb 12:28** *Wherefore **we receiving a kingdom** which cannot be moved,(L) let us have grace, whereby we may serve God acceptably with reverence and godly fear: (N)*
- **Jas 2:5** *Hearken, my beloved brethren, Hath not God chosen the poor of this world rich in faith, and **heirs of the kingdom which he hath promised** to them that love him?*
- **2Pe 1:11** *For so an **entrance shall be ministered unto you abundantly into the everlasting kingdom** of our Lord and Saviour Jesus Christ.*

#2 We, who have suffered with Christ here and faithfully finished our course, will reign with Him over other people. Zechariah 14 seems to say it will be those left after Christ conquers this world; and Rev. 5:10 says it will be on this earth.

■ **Zech 14:16** *And it shall come to pass,* **that every one that is left of all the nations which came against Jerusalem** *shall even go up from year to year to worship the King, the LORD of hosts, and to keep the feast of tabernacles.* 17 *And it shall be, that whoso will not come up of all the families of the earth unto Jerusalem to worship the King, the LORD of hosts,* **even upon them shall be no rain.**

■ **Mt 19:27** *Then answered Peter and said unto him, Behold, we have forsaken all, and followed thee; what shall we have therefore? 28 And Jesus said unto them, Verily I say unto you, That ye which have followed me,* **in the regeneration** *when the Son of man shall sit in the throne of his glory, ye also shall sit upon twelve thrones, judging the twelve tribes of Israel.*

■ **Lu 22:28** *Ye are they which have continued with me in my temptations. 29 And I appoint unto you a kingdom, as my Father hath appointed unto me; 30 That ye may eat and drink at my table in my kingdom, and sit on thrones judging the twelve tribes of Israel.*

■ **1Co 6:2** *Do ye not know that the saints shall judge the world? and if the world shall be judged by you, are ye unworthy to judge the smallest matters?*

■ **2 Tim 2:11** *It is a faithful saying: For if we be dead with him, we shall also live with him: 12* **If we suffer, we shall also reign with him:** *if we deny him, he also will deny us:*

■ **Re 2:26** *And he that overcometh, and keepeth my works unto the end, to him will I give* **power over the nations:** *27 And* **he shall rule them with a rod of iron; as the vessels of a potter shall they be broken to shivers:** *even as I received of my Father.*

■ **Re 5:10** *And hast made us unto our God kings and priests: and* **we shall reign on the earth.** (compare Zech 14:16)

#3 Christ's Throne is called the Throne of his father David. Christ is called the "Son of David". This Kingdom is future.

■ **Mt 25:31** *When the Son of man shall come in his glory, and all the holy angels with him,* **then shall he sit upon the throne of his glory:**
■ **Lu 1:32** *He shall be great, and shall be called the Son of the Highest:* **and the Lord God shall give unto him the throne of his father David:**
■ **Ac 2:30** *Therefore being a prophet, and knowing that God had sworn with an oath to him, that of the fruit of his loins, according to the flesh,* **he would raise up Christ to sit on his throne;**

#4 We are now to spread the glad tidings of this coming kingdom, preach the principles upon which it is built, and call men to the hope and preparation for it. We are now in the highways and hedges compelling people to come to the wedding.

■ **Mt 22:9** *Go ye therefore into the highways, and as many as ye shall find,* **bid to the marriage.**
■ **Lu 8:1** *And it came to pass afterward, that he went throughout every city and village,* **preaching and shewing the glad tidings of the kingdom of God:** *and the twelve were with him,*
■ **Ac 8:12** *But when they believed Philip preaching the things* **concerning the kingdom of God,** *and the name of Jesus Christ, they were baptized, both men and women.*
■ **Ac 14:22** *Confirming the souls of the disciples, and exhorting them to* **continue in the faith, and that we**

149

must through much tribulation enter into the kingdom of God.

■ *Ac 19:8 And he went into the synagogue, and spake boldly for the space of three months, **disputing and persuading the things concerning the kingdom of God.***

■ *Ac 20:25 And now, behold, I know that ye all, among whom I have gone preaching the kingdom of God, shall see my face no more.*

■ *Ac 28:23 And when they had appointed him a day, there came many to him into his lodging; to whom he expounded and **testified the kingdom of God, persuading them concerning Jesus, both out of the law of Moses, and out of the prophets,** from morning till evening.*

Notice that Paul preached the kingdom of God out of the Law of Moses and the prophets – this is the Bible that they had. This proves that the kingdom of God is not some radical new idea of the New Testament in contradistinction to the Old Testament.

Now, with these definite principles in mind, let us consider a few things. If there is coming a kingdom where the "Just One" will reign with a Rod of Iron; will enforce righteousness on the earth; will reign on the throne of his father David; will have His saints reigning with him; etc....And, If we are now to be proclaiming the glories and hopes of this King and Kingdom, so men will repent and prepare their hearts for the coming King....And, If we are seen now as ambassadors for this coming kingdom of righteousness....where does pacifism come in? It simply doesn't fit; and the church of Jesus Christ on earth now is not THE kingdom; but is waiting for, preparing for, and preaching the coming kingdom. The church is betrothed as the King's Bride; but the marriage has not taken place. We are therefore in some degree in His realm, His "kingdom"; but not in the full sense. IF what we have now is a taste and foreshadowing of the coming kingdom, THEN THERE SHOULD BE NO MATERIAL DIFFERENCE IN THE FOUNDATIONAL PRINCIPLES.

It is prophesied that the peace Jesus brings on the earth with His sword and rod will cause the nations to cease fearing the threat of danger, so they will beat their swords into plowshares and their spears into pruning hooks, and will learn war no more - not because they are pacifists, but because they are SAFE under Christ's reign. Can you imagine living on this earth with Christ reigning from Jerusalem? This is the hope of the believer as I understand the Bible.

■ *Isa 2:4 And he shall judge among the nations, and shall rebuke many people: and they shall beat their swords into plowshares, and their spears into pruninghooks: **nation** shall not lift up sword against **nation,** neither shall they learn war any more.*

■ *Isa 9:6 For unto us a child is born, unto us a son is given: and the government shall be upon his shoulder: and his name shall be called Wonderful, Counsellor, The mighty God, The everlasting Father, The Prince of Peace. 7 Of the increase of his government and peace there shall be no end, upon the throne of David, and upon his kingdom, to order it, and to establish it with judgment and with justice from henceforth even for ever. The zeal of the LORD of hosts will perform this.*

■ *Mic 4:1 But in the last days it shall come to pass, that the mountain of the house of the LORD shall be established in the top of the mountains, and it shall be exalted above the hills; and people shall flow unto it.*

151

*2And many **nations** shall come, and say, Come, and let us go up to the mountain of the LORD, and to the house of the God of Jacob; and he will teach us of his ways, and we will walk in his paths: for the law shall go forth of Zion, and the word of the LORD from Jerusalem. 3 And **he shall judge among many people, and rebuke strong <u>nations</u> afar off; and they shall beat their swords into plowshares, and their spears into pruninghooks: <u>nation</u> shall not lift up a sword against <u>nation</u>, neither shall they learn war any more.** 4 But they shall sit every man under his vine and under his fig tree; and **<u>none shall make them afraid</u>**: for the mouth of the LORD of hosts hath spoken it. (See also Zech 14)*

We know this is not speaking of the church age, because Jesus said the following concerning the church age, which we are presently in:

■ ***Mt. 24: 4*** *And Jesus answered and said unto them, Take heed that no man deceive you. 5 For many shall come in my name, saying, I am Christ; and shall deceive many. 6 And **ye shall hear of wars and rumours of wars:** see that ye be not troubled: for all these things must come to pass, but the end is not yet. 7 **For nation shall rise against nation, and kingdom against kingdom:** and there shall be famines, and pestilences, and earthquakes, in divers places. 8 All these are the beginning of sorrows. 9 Then shall they deliver you up to be afflicted, and shall kill you: and ye shall be hated of all nations for my name's sake. 10 And then shall many be offended, and shall betray one another, and shall hate one another. 11 And many false prophets shall rise, and shall deceive many. 12 And because iniquity shall abound, the love of many shall wax cold. 13 But he that shall endure unto the end, the same shall be saved. 14 And **this gospel of the kingdom shall be preached in all the world for a witness unto all nations; and then shall the end come.***

We are in this age of turmoil waiting for the coming Kingdom of Christ. We are to be preaching the glad tidings of this kingdom. We are ambassadors for the coming kingdom, and therefore need to study and learn what is expected of us.

In Revelation we see this scenario laid out for us:

■ The "Israel of God" brings forth the Messiah, who is caught up to heaven: (Acts 3:21)

Re 12:5 And she brought forth a man child, who was to rule all nations with a rod of iron: and her child was caught up unto God, and to his throne.

■ The "Church" flees to the wilderness and Christians are persecuted by Satan who knows he has a short time left.

Re 12:11 And they overcame him by the blood of the Lamb, and by the word of their testimony; and they loved not their lives unto the death. 12 Therefore rejoice, ye heavens, and ye that dwell in them. Woe to the inhabiters of the earth and of the sea! for the devil is come down unto you, having great wrath, because he knoweth that he hath but a short time.

■ The gospel is preached around the world:

Re 14:6 ¶ And I saw another angel fly in the midst of heaven, having the everlasting gospel to preach unto them that dwell on the earth, and to every nation, and kindred, and tongue, and people,

■ Jesus (the child brought forth by the woman) returns to judge, conquer, and reign with the rod of iron (see also Zech 14)

Re 19:11 And I saw heaven opened, and behold a white horse; and he that sat upon him was called Faithful and True, and in righteousness he doth judge and make war. 12 His eyes were as a flame of fire, and on his head were many crowns; and he had a name written, that no man knew, but he himself. 13 And he was clothed with a vesture dipped in blood: and his name is called The Word of God.

■ Believers who have died or were caught up come with Him will judge and reign (Jude 14,15; 1Th 4:17)

Re 19:14 And the armies which were in heaven followed him upon white horses, clothed in fine linen, white and clean. 15 And out of his mouth goeth a sharp sword, that with it he should smite the nations: and he shall rule them with a rod of iron: and he treadeth the winepress of the fierceness and wrath of Almighty God. 16 And he hath on his vesture and on his thigh a name written, KING OF KINGS, AND LORD OF LORDS.

■ In Revelation 20 we see Satan bound for 1000 years while Jesus and His saints reign on the earth over mortals. We see that these people are mortals who can still be deceived and rebel against Christ when Satan is loosed.

Re 20: 1 ¶ And I saw an angel come down from heaven, having the key of the bottomless pit and a great chain in his hand. 2 And he laid hold on the dragon, that old serpent, which is the Devil, and Satan, and bound him a thousand years, 3 And cast him into the bottomless pit, and shut him up, and set a seal upon him, that he should deceive the nations no more, till the thousand years should be fulfilled: and after that he must be loosed a little season. 4 And I saw thrones, and they sat upon them, and judgment was given unto them: and I saw the souls of them that were beheaded for the witness of Jesus, and for the word of God, and which had not worshipped the beast, neither his image, neither had received his mark upon their foreheads, or in their hands; and they lived and reigned with Christ a thousand years. 5 But the rest of the dead lived not again until the thousand years were finished. This is the first resurrection. 6 Blessed and holy is he that hath part in the first resurrection: on such the second death hath no power, but they shall be priests of God and of Christ, and shall reign with him a thousand years. 7 And when the thousand years are expired, Satan shall be loosed out of his prison, 8 And shall go out to deceive the nations which are in the four quarters of the earth, Gog and Magog, to gather them together to battle: the number of whom is as the sand of the sea. 9 And they went up on the breadth of the earth, and compassed the camp of the saints about, and the beloved city: and fire came down from God out of heaven, and devoured them. 10 And the devil that deceived them was cast into the lake of fire and brimstone, where the beast and the false prophet are, and shall be tormented day and night for ever and ever.

■ After the 1000 year reign we see the final judgment:

Re 20:11 ¶ And I saw a great white throne, and him that sat on it, from whose face the earth and the heaven fled away; and there was found no place for them. 12 And I saw the dead, small and great, stand before God; and the books were opened: and another book was opened, which is the book of life: and the dead were judged out of those things which were written in the books, according to their works. 13 And the sea gave up the dead which were in it; and death and hell delivered up the dead which were in them: and they were judged every man according to their works. 14 And death and hell were cast into the lake of fire. This is the second death. 15 And whosoever was not found written in the book of life was cast into the lake of fire.

So, we are supposed to be representing this coming King and Kingdom by proclaiming the glories and virtues of both. We are to proclaim the justice and righteousness of this coming kingdom as a standard and pattern for present men and governments. We are to represent to men the rightness and appropriateness of our King's ways, and His claim upon men and the earth. We are to call men to now repent and accept Him as their King, or face His wrath for their rebellion. This opportunity to repent and reconcile is the Gospel message we are to preach along with the glad tidings of the coming Kingdom of righteousness.

We need to preach what the Bible says about righteousness in all of life including government, so men know what Jesus' reign will be like. We need to preach all the realms of holiness that will be active and operating in Christ's future kingdom while we pray, "Thy kingdom come, thy will be done on earth as it is in heaven".

Friend, where will you be when Jesus returns? Will you have been faithfully doing his work and service? Will you be the unfaithful servant who thought he could get by on minimum effort? Many are banking on that fallacy today! They are hoping to slip into Christ's Kingdom on minimum effort with their Lord's money buried in the earth.

Will you be one who declared by his life, "I will not have this man to reign over me"? Those who were not ready when the lord returned were actually banking on the possibility that he may not return.

Only those doing what their master said could claim that they believed in his return after having received the kingdom. What was the main thing that stumbled those who were waiting for the coming of Christ, according to His parables?

Mt. 24:42 Watch therefore: for ye know not what hour your Lord doth come. 43 But know this, that if the goodman of the house had known in what watch the thief would come, he would have watched, and would not have suffered his house to be broken up. 44 Therefore be ye also ready: for in such an hour as ye think not the Son of man cometh. 45 Who then is a faithful and wise servant, whom his lord hath made ruler over his household, to give them meat in due season? 46 Blessed is that servant, whom his lord when he cometh shall find so doing. 47 Verily I say unto you, That he shall make him ruler over all his goods. 48 But and if that evil servant shall say in his heart, **My lord delayeth his coming;** *49 And shall begin to smite his fellowservants, and to eat and drink with the drunken; 50 The lord of that servant shall come in a day when he looketh not for him, and in an hour that he is not aware of, 51 And shall cut him asunder, and appoint him his portion with the hypocrites: there shall be weeping and gnashing of teeth.*

DELAY! That seems to be the greatest stumbling stone. Consider the foolish virgins. The only thing that tripped them up was the delay. They were not ready for the long haul. They were not prepared for **DELAY**. Are you? Are you ready for 30, 40, or 50 years of faithful obedience through tribulation and suffering?

157

*Lu 12:32 Fear not, little flock; for it is your Father's good pleasure to give you the kingdom. 33 Sell that ye have, and give alms; provide yourselves bags which wax not old, a treasure in the heavens that faileth not, where no thief approacheth, neither moth corrupteth. 34 For where your treasure is, there will your heart be also. 35 Let your loins be girded about, and your lights burning; 36 And ye yourselves like unto men that wait for their lord, when he will return from the wedding; that when he cometh and knocketh, they may open unto him immediately. 37 Blessed are those servants, whom the lord when he cometh shall find watching: verily I say unto you, that he shall gird himself, and make them to sit down to meat, and will come forth and serve them. 38 **And if he shall come in the second watch, or come in the third watch, and find them so, blessed are those servants.** 39 And this know, that if the goodman of the house had known what hour the thief would come, he would have watched, and not have suffered his house to be broken through. 40 Be ye therefore ready also: for the Son of man cometh at an hour when ye think not.*

Mt 25:19 After a **long time** *the lord of those servants cometh, and reckoneth with them.*

What is Jesus telling us? Is this not a clear indication of a time of **delay**? Listen to what Jesus says again:

*Lu 18:7 And shall not God avenge his own elect, which cry day and night unto him, __though he bear long with them?__ 8 I tell you that he will avenge them speedily. **Nevertheless when the Son of man cometh, shall he find faith on the earth?***

Why would he not find faith on the earth? Well, the whole purpose of the parable in Luke 18:1-8 is *"that men ought always to pray, and not to faint;"* This seems to be dealing with the same issue i.e. that men faint and lose their faith when the Lord seems to **DELAY** his answers and the fulfillment of His promises. Extended TIME becomes an intense test of faithfulness.

Peter gives us an exhortation to the same end, and reveals that the scoffers in the last days will take advantage of this seeming delay.

> **2Pe 3:3** *Knowing this first, that there shall come in the last days scoffers, walking after their own lusts, 4 And saying,* **Where is the promise of his coming? for since the fathers fell asleep, all things continue as they were from the beginning of the creation.** *5 For this they willingly are ignorant of, that by the word of God the heavens were of old, and the earth standing out of the water and in the water: 6 Whereby the world that then was, being overflowed with water, perished: 7 But the heavens and the earth, which are now, by the same word are kept in store, reserved unto fire against the day of judgment and perdition of ungodly men. 8 But, beloved, be not ignorant of this one thing, that one day is with the Lord as a thousand years, and a thousand years as one day. 9* **The Lord is not slack concerning his promise, as some men count slackness; but is longsuffering to us-ward, not willing that any should perish, but that all should come to repentance.** *10 But the day of the Lord will come as a thief in the night;*

God may seem slow, but He is never late! He will not be slack concerning His promise, but will be right on time, just like Jesus was in His first advent. The question Jesus had was whether or not He would find faith on the earth. Will He find you exercising a living obeying faith in a biblical hope? *Time will tell.*

> *2Th 3:5* And the Lord direct your hearts into the love of God, and into the **patient waiting for Christ.**

Chapter 13

Cure For The Calvinist Cancer

There is a principle in Scripture which would cure much heresy if people could only comprehend it. Once understood, this truth of God's Word would annihilate the TULIP of the Calvinist and would straighten out all false interpretations of Scripture concerning God's calling, election, predestination, and grace. What is the down side? Men who love their creed more than God's truth continue to close their eyes and minds to this principle and thus continue to spout their errors to lead astray and confuse the unwary.

So what is this miracle cure? Is it well established in Scripture? Does God make it really plain? Yes, indeed. God repeats this over and over in Scripture many times in many ways; and if men would just believe His testimony of His own character, they would not continually interpret the Scriptures contrary to it. Observe:

De 10:17 *For the LORD your God is God of gods, and Lord of lords, a great God, a mighty, and a terrible, which **regardeth not persons**, nor taketh reward:*

2Ch 19:7 *Wherefore now let the fear of the LORD be upon you; take heed and do it: for there is no iniquity with the LORD our God, **nor respect of persons**, nor taking of gifts.*

161

Ac 10:34 *Then Peter opened his mouth, and said, Of a truth I perceive that* **God is no respecter of persons:**

Ga 2:6 *But of these who seemed to be somewhat, (whatsoever they were, it maketh no matter to me:* **God accepteth no man's person***:) for they who seemed to be somewhat in conference added nothing to me:*

Eph 6:9 *And, ye masters, do the same things unto them, forbearing threatening: knowing that your Master also is in heaven;* **neither is there respect of persons with him.**

Col 3:25 *But he that doeth wrong shall receive for the wrong which he hath done: and* **there is no respect of persons.**

1Ti 5:21 *I charge thee before God, and the Lord Jesus Christ, and the elect angels, that thou observe these things without preferring one before another,* **doing nothing by partiality.**

Jas 2:1 *My brethren,* **have not** *the faith of our Lord Jesus Christ, the Lord of glory,* **with respect of persons***...**Jas 2:4** Are ye not then* **partial in yourselves***, and are become* **judges of evil thoughts***? ...**Jas 2:9** But* **if ye have respect to persons, ye commit sin,** *and are* **convinced of the law as transgressors***. ...**Jas 3:17** But the wisdom that is from above is first pure, then peaceable, gentle, and easy to be intreated, full of mercy and good fruits,* **without partiality, and without hypocrisy.**

1Pe 1:17 *And if ye call on the Father,* **who without respect of persons judgeth according to every man's work,** *pass the time of your sojourning here in fear:*

Now listen close to the apostle as he explains the impartial and perfectly just judgment of God. If men would simply believe what Paul is saying here, they would never interpret Romans 9 in their foolish and erroneous Calvinistic way.

*Rom 2:5 ...the **righteous** judgment of God; **Who will render to every man according to his deeds:** 7 To them who by patient continuance in well doing seek for glory and honour and immortality, eternal life: 8 But unto them that are contentious, and do not obey the truth, but obey unrighteousness, indignation and wrath, 9 Tribulation and anguish, upon every soul of man that doeth evil, **of the Jew first, and also of the Gentile;** 10 But glory, honour, and peace, to every man that worketh good, **to the Jew first, and also to the Gentile:** 11 **For there is no respect of persons with God.***

God IS A RESPECTER OF DEEDS – NOT PERSONS!

*Rev 22:12 And, behold, I come quickly; and my reward is with me, to give **every man according as his work shall be.***

Could God say this if some men received special help while others did not?? What does this mean? This means that men going to heaven or hell; having God's grace or wrath; being the elected or rejected; and men being saved or lost is wholly and completely dependent upon their actions and choices without any partiality on God's part – PERIOD! If God chooses to save or help one man over another man simply due to favoring the one over the other; then God is committing sin, transgressing His own Law, and His Word is a lie. When God determines who goes to heaven and who goes to hell it cannot be based on God making it easier for one person over another or helping one more than the other or choosing one over the other. This would be "respect of persons" and would be sin according to God's Law.

163

Listen close: Even if God knows what men will do before they do it, He cannot base any of His actions towards them on this knowledge or it is respect of persons in judgment -- prejudice. If God helped someone over another with partiality, then His foreknowledge could only be that they did better because He showed partiality – Thus God electing and helping someone due to foreknowledge is impossible! He can only have foreknowledge of what actually would happen not what never did happen! That means if he knows a man, like in Luke 8:13, is receiving the Word with joy; but will not endure to the end, God STILL TREATS HIM THE SAME AS ANY OTHER MAN WHO RECEIVES THE WORD WITH JOY AND DOES NOT WITHHOLD GRACE OR HELP JUST BECAUSE HE KNOWS THE MAN WILL FALL AWAY SOMEDAY AND NOT CONTINUE TO THE END. If God helped one endure whom "He knew would endure" then God only knew He would endure because God helped him endure because God knew He would endure............So God chooses the elect based on what? On foreknowledge? Of WHAT? Foreknowledge that they endured because they were the elect? If they endured because they were the elect, then the only foreknowledge God could have is that they endured because they were the elect. God can only foreknow what really happened in the future. If God foreknew that I would endure, so He helps me more, then what did He foreknow? That I would endure without His help? Is that why He helped me? This is impossible, because if He helps me He changes the future and His foreknowledge

164

was a myth ---- Do you see the impossibility of all this foolishness???? Can you see the foolishness in all this?

God gives more grace to every man who properly uses the grace already given and this is perfectly just; but God will not give grace to someone just because He "chose" or "elected" them to eternal life based on nothing of their own actions. That would be "respect of persons" in judgment. If God knows I will endure to the end, then He knows I will endure to the end without Him showing partiality or favoritism towards me and NOT BECAUSE HE DID. He is not a hypocrite or a liar. Why would God keep any man from falling away more than He did Adam and Eve? That would be respect of persons; and God would never do that.   If God didn't keep Adam and Eve from falling, then He is not going to keep you or any other man from falling, except with the same degree of help He gave Adam and Eve.

God does not play "favorites"! It is indelibly written in the constitution of the universe that THERE IS NO RESPECT OF PERSONS WITH GOD.   God does not show partiality in His judgment of men.   Do you believe this?   Do you understand this? Once you understand this, you cannot believe any of the concepts of Calvinistic election or predestination.

But what do the verses mean that men use to imply such actions on God's part? There are clear explanations for all such verses which do not cause any contradictions. The Apostles were not senile; but inspired by the Father with whom is no variableness, neither shadow of turning. An unchanging God is perfectly consistent throughout His revelation of Himself to man. Many times the Bible clearly says that God's judgment is without partiality, so that must be our basis for belief in God's judgment. If you interpret contrary to that principle, then you are slandering God and rejecting His clear Word concerning Himself.

Now, listen close: Notice in Romans 2, where God's judgment is clearly explained, that it says, "To the Jew first and also to the Gentile" concerning both grace and wrath. What makes the distinction between Jews and Gentiles? It was God's choosing Abraham's seed as a special people to himself for His purpose of bringing the Messiah into the World for the redemption of all mankind. For God to make a covenant with Abraham to show special favor to his descendents because Abraham believed and obeyed God (Gen 26:5), is not "respect of persons" in judgment. Why? HOW? Because when it came to the salvation or damnation of individuals those with greater opportunity were also judged more harshly for not properly making use of their greater privileges. This is what Paul is clearly showing in Romans 2. Because of Abraham's obedience, the Jews had greater opportunities to know and hear God's Word; but they also had greater judgment for not taking this opportunity; which clearly shows God's justice in His offer of salvation to man. Read it again:

*Rom 2:5 ...the righteous judgment of God; Who will render to **every man according to his deeds:** 7 To them who by patient* *continuance in well doing seek for glory and honour and immortality, eternal life: 8 But unto them that are contentious, and do not obey the truth, but obey unrighteousness, indignation and wrath, 9 Tribulation and anguish, upon every soul of man that doeth evil, of **the Jew first, and also of the Gentile**; 10 But glory, honour, and peace, to every man that worketh good, **to the Jew first, and also to the Gentile:** 11 **For there is no respect of persons with God.** 12 For as many as have sinned without law shall also perish without law: and as many as have sinned in the law shall be judged by the law; 13 (For not the hearers of the law are just before God, but the doers of the law shall be justified. 14 For when the Gentiles, which have not the law, do by nature the things contained in the law, these, having not the law, are a law unto themselves: 15 Which shew the work of the law written in their hearts, their conscience also bearing witness, and their thoughts the mean while accusing or else excusing one another;) 16 In the day when God shall judge the secrets of men by Jesus Christ according to my gospel.*

Jews and Gentiles both had light and could have received greater light. God's judgment concerning salvation or damnation is based on "What you did with what you had from where you were at". This is perfectly appropriate without any partiality. "What did you do with the light you had?" is the primary question in God's judgment. God's foreknowledge could not tamper with or affect this outcome at all; but God's impartial judgment must allow all men to exercise their free will and eat the fruit of their own choices. They all have the ability to repent and walk in the light God has given them to the salvation of their souls.

*Ga 6:7 Be not deceived; God is not mocked: for **whatsoever a man soweth, that shall he also reap**. 8 For he that soweth to his flesh shall of the flesh reap corruption; but he that soweth to the Spirit shall of the Spirit reap life everlasting.*

*Titus 2:11 For the grace of God that bringeth salvation <u>**hath appeared to all men,**</u> 12 Teaching us that, denying ungodliness and worldly lusts, we should live soberly, righteously, and godly, in this present world;*

*Joh 1:1 In the beginning was the Word, and the Word was with God, and the Word was God. 2 The same was in the beginning with God. 3 All things were made by him; and without him was not any thing made that was made. 4 In him was life; and the life was the light of men. 5 And the light shineth in darkness; and the darkness comprehended it not. 6 There was a man sent from God, whose name was John. 7 The same came for a witness, to bear witness of the Light, that all men through him might believe. 8 He was not that Light, but was sent to bear witness of that Light. 9 **That was the true Light, which lighteth <u>every</u> man that cometh into the world.** 10 He was in the world, and the world was made by him, and the world knew him not. 11 He came unto his own, and his own received him not. 12 **But <u>as many as received him</u>, to them gave he power to become the sons of God, even to them that believe on his name:***

This refers to Jews and Gentiles alike. They both could be saved; but one group had greater privileges due to being chosen as the vehicle through which the Messiah would come into the World.

*Joh 3:16 For God so loved the **world**, that he gave his only begotten Son, that **whosoever** believeth in him should not perish, but have everlasting life.*

Since God promised Abraham that the Messiah would come through his seed, God also had the responsibility to pick which of Abraham's descendents would be used. Did this affect whether they could be saved or not? No, but it affected what opportunities and privileges they would have to know God. The greater the opportunity, the greater the judgment – why? Because this is what makes it perfectly just. If I improve my opportunities and seek God more than my neighbor, then I receive more grace and light to pass on to my children. My children then have a greater opportunity to know God than my neighbor's; but they are also more accountable to God to walk in the greater light they have. Salvation and grace will be to my children first, and also to my neighbor's; but judgment will be to my children first and also to my neighbor's – FOR THERE IS NO RESPECT OF PERSONS WITH GOD.

*1Pe 4:17 For the time is come that **judgment must begin at the house of God:** and if it first begin at us, what shall the end be of them that obey not the gospel of God? 18 And if the righteous scarcely be saved, where shall the ungodly and the sinner appear? 19 Wherefore let them that suffer according to the will of God **commit the keeping of their souls to him in well doing,** as unto a faithful Creator.*

"Faithful" refers to His justice. Since God is no respecter of persons and does not play "favorites", He must demand more from those to whom more is given. God is free to choose people; people groups; nations; etc. for special purposes in His redemption plan as long as "to whom much is given, much is required" so that God is no

169

respecter of persons concerning individual people's salvation. This is perfectly fair and just.

In the Scriptures we find that God deals with nations and people groups in a similar fashion as He deals with individuals. We see God declaring this fact in Jeremiah 18.

Jer 18:1 ¶ The word which came to Jeremiah from the LORD, saying, 2 Arise, and go down to the potter's house, and there I will cause thee to hear my words. 3 Then I went down to the potter's house, and, behold, he wrought a work on the wheels. 4 And the vessel that he made of clay was marred in the hand of the potter: so he made it again another vessel, as seemed good to the potter to make it. 5 Then the word of the LORD came to me, saying, 6 O house of Israel, cannot I do with you as this potter? saith the LORD. Behold, as the clay is in the potter's hand, so are ye in mine hand, O house of Israel. 7 At what instant I shall speak concerning a nation, and concerning a kingdom, to pluck up, and to pull down, and to destroy it; 8 If that nation, against whom I have pronounced, turn from their evil, I will repent of the evil that I thought to do unto them. 9 And at what instant I shall speak concerning a nation, and concerning a kingdom, to build and to plant it; 10 If it do evil in my sight, that it obey not my voice, then I will repent of the good, wherewith I said I would benefit them.

In Romans 9 the Calvinists completely set Paul in contradiction to what he declared in Romans 2; but any honest Bible interpreter knows this is foolishness. God is not declaring his freedom to show respect of persons; but justifying His giving the special privileges promised to Abraham's seed to the Church in the light of the FACT

THAT HE DOES NOT HAVE RESPECT TO PERSONS. He even refers to Jeremiah 18 and the principle there as part of his reasoning. In Romans 9 Paul is dealing with a completely different issue than in Romans 2. In chapter 2 Paul is dealing clearly with the salvation or damnation of individuals; but in chapter 9 Paul is speaking of God's dealings with NATIONS and PEOPLE GROUPS for God's redemption program. Every name given in Romans 9 is the head of a people group – Abraham, Isaac, Jacob, Esau, and Pharaoh – and they are clearly used in that sense alone.

*Ge 25:23 And the LORD said unto her, Two **nations** are in thy womb, and **two manner of people** shall be separated from thy bowels; and the **one people shall be stronger than the other people;** and the elder shall serve the younger.*

Paul is using them in this way to show forth the principle spoken of in Jeremiah 18 which we just read. *"Jacob have I loved, but Esau have I hated"* is quoting Malachi, the last book of the Old Testament and is only referring to the descendents – Edom and Israel. This means God chose to work through Israel and not Edom, but God did bless and look after Esau's descendents until they became wicked – Read Deuteronomy chapter 2. God gave them Mt. Seir and drove out the giants for them as He did for Israel; and did not allow Israel to take their land. Jacob personally never served Esau one day; but rather called him "lord".

Paul is explaining how God's promise to Abraham's seed and the privileges conferred thereby are being continued now through the Church of Jesus Christ (a people group) and no longer through the nation of Israel. God chose to work through the nation of Israel due to no righteousness or "works" of their own, but due to God's own mercy and promises to Abraham, Isaac, and Jacob – This is what Romans 9:11 is referring to and is speaking of the nations, not the "children" themselves – The word "children" is not in the Greek.

De 9:4 *Speak not thou in thine heart, after that the LORD thy God hath cast them out from before thee, saying, For my righteousness the LORD hath brought me in to possess this land: but for the wickedness of these nations the LORD doth drive them out from before thee. 5* **Not for thy righteousness**, *or for the uprightness of thine heart, dost thou go to possess their land: but for the wickedness of these nations the LORD thy God doth drive them out from before thee, and* **that he may perform the word which the LORD sware unto thy fathers, Abraham, Isaac, and Jacob**. *6 Understand therefore,* **that the LORD thy God giveth thee not this good land to possess it for thy righteousness**; *for thou art a stiffnecked people.*

The Church qualifies as the fulfillment of "in Isaac shall thy seed be called" because this promise was to those with the "faith of Abraham", not just physical descendants. The Church is the Spiritual element of Israel with believing Gentiles grafted in. Jesus is said in Galatians 3:16 to be the "seed", and thus all under His administration by faith in Him now qualify for the children of Abraham and the blessings promised. They are the "Israel of God" (Ga 6)

These privileges "pertained" to Israel the nation (Ro 9:4) – were predetermined for them as the elect of God; but they were unfaithful and so now the faithful remnant, who received Christ as Messiah, along with believing Gentiles are now God's special people group to work through and Israel as a nation would soon be destroyed (AD 70). Individuals within these two groups can still be saved or lost; but a new people group and program is now in place. God told them that this would happen so that all those who really cared and loved God would be ready for it.

*Rom 9:25 ¶ As he saith also in Osee, **I will call them my people, which were not my people; and her beloved, which was not beloved**. 26 And it shall come to pass, that in the place where it was said unto them, Ye are not my people; there shall they be called the children of the living God. 27 Esaias also crieth concerning Israel, **Though the number of the children of Israel be as the sand of the sea, a remnant shall be saved**: 28 For he will finish the work, and cut it short in righteousness **[IMPARTIAL JUSTICE]**: because a short work will the Lord make upon the earth. 29 And as Esaias said before, Except the Lord of Sabaoth had left us a seed, we had been as Sodoma, and been made like unto Gomorrha. 30 **What shall we say then? That the Gentiles, which followed not after righteousness, have attained to righteousness, even the righteousness which is of faith. 31 But Israel, which followed after the law of righteousness, hath not attained to the law of righteousness. 32 <u>Wherefore? Because they sought it not by faith, but as it were by the works of the law. For they stumbled at that stumblingstone;</u>***

Ro 9:32 above, is what Paul is referring to when he says, *"So then it is not of him that willeth, nor of him that runneth, but of God that sheweth mercy".* Israel willed and ran to establish their own righteousness just as Esau did to obtain a birthright which he had despised; but they were not in line with God's mercy because they were going about to establish their own program and not submitting to God's program (Ro 10:1-3).

Israel was at one time a vessel receiving God's mercy and God used Egypt (Pharaoh) who became a vessel of wrath to birth the nation of Israel. In the same way God has endured Israel who became a vessel of wrath to birth the Church which is now God's vessel of mercy. The Church is God's people group including both Jews and Gentiles who believe and obey Jesus. The salvation or damnation of the people in these nations or groups is still individually determined with NO RESPECT OF PERSONS. Just as people in Egypt could be saved when Egypt was a vessel of wrath and people in Israel could be damned while the nation was a vessel of mercy; so people could be saved in Israel as a vessel of wrath and people in the Church could fall away and be damned though living in the privileged people group (Acts 5:1-11) – the Church – the vessel of mercy. Esau could have been saved as a circumcised son of Abraham as well as Ishmael or any of their descendents; but God's choice for the nation which would birth the Messiah was through Isaac and Jacob. Did this ensure the salvation of all of Isaac and Jacob's descendents? Of course not. We know many were not saved.

The Bible is very clear that God predetermined a program for the salvation of mankind from the beginning of the world. He knew that Adam and Eve could fall and considered what He would do if they did. He set up a plan of WHAT He would do and WHAT REQUIREMENTS WERE NECESSARY for Him to righteously reconcile with repentant sinners. In the mind of God the over-all plan was laid; but there is no indication that God chose some people to salvation and some to damnation prior to their existence. So what do the verses mean that people use to teach this? Let's look at a number of verses that are misused in this way:

Joh 6:44 No man can come to me, except the Father which hath sent me draw him: and I will raise him up at the last day. 45 It is written in the prophets, And they shall be all taught of God. Every man therefore that hath heard, and hath learned of the Father, cometh unto me.

Men use this passage to teach that God MAKES some people come to Christ and neglects others; but any honest reader can see the verse 45 explains the justice of the situation. God is calling and drawing ALL men; but only those who HEAR and LEARN from the light God shines will actually come to Jesus as Messiah.

Those Jews whose hearts were keeping pace with the light God had shined on the whole nation recognized Jesus as their Messiah – came to Him. There is no RESPECT OF PERSONS in this scenario. Jesus declares the same thing in a couple of places:

Joh 5:46 For had ye believed Moses, ye would have believed me: for he wrote of me.

Lu 16:31 And he said unto him, If they hear not Moses and the prophets, neither will they be persuaded, though one rose from the dead.

This is perfectly consistent with God's just dealings with man. This principle can be seen in another passage which people misuse.

Ac 13:48 And when the Gentiles heard this, they were glad, and glorified the word of the Lord: and as many as were ordained to eternal life believed.

The word "ordained" here simply means they were "predisposed" to believing due to "hearing and learning" of the Father. God "foreknew" them and their hearts because His Spirit had already been working with all of them since they came to the age of accountability. God's Spirit strives with all men. He even strove with those who died in the flood; but finally gave up on them (Gen 6:1-8). These people were "in line" to believe because they were not prejudiced against believing nor hardened against God's light as many of the Jews were.

- **ADAM CLARKE:** Verse 48. *[As many as were ordained to eternal life believed.]* This text has been most pitifully misunderstood. Many suppose that it simply means that those in that assembly who were fore-ordained; or predestinated by God's decree, to eternal life, believed under the influence of that decree. Now, we should be careful to examine what a word means, before we attempt to fix its meaning. Whatever tetagmenoi may mean, which is the word we translate ordained, it is neither protetagmenoi nor proorismenoi which the apostle uses, but simply tetagmenoi, which includes no idea of pre-ordination or pre-destination of any kind. And if it even did, it would be rather hazardous to say that all those who believed at this time were such as actually persevered unto the end, and were saved unto eternal life. But, leaving all these precarious matters, what does the word tetagmenov mean? The verb tattw or tassw signifies to place, set, order, appoint, dispose; hence it has been considered here as implying the disposition or readiness of mind of several persons in the congregation, such as the religious proselytes mentioned Ac 13:43, who possessed the reverse of the disposition of those Jews who spake against those things, contradicting and blaspheming, Ac 13:45. Though the word in this place has been variously translated, yet, of all the meanings ever put on it, none agrees worse with its nature and known signification than that which represents it as intending those who were predestinated to eternal life: this is no meaning of the term, and should never be applied to it. Let us, without prejudice, consider the scope of the place: the Jews contradicted and blasphemed; the religious proselytes heard attentively, and received the word of life: the one party were utterly indisposed, through their own stubbornness, to receive the Gospel; the others, destitute of prejudice and prepossession, were glad to hear that, in the order of God, the

Gentiles were included in the covenant of salvation through Christ Jesus; they, therefore, in this good state and order of mind, believed. Those who seek for the plain meaning of the word will find it here: those who wish to make out a sense, not from the Greek word, its use among the best Greek writers, and the obvious sense of the evangelist, but from their own creed, may continue to puzzle themselves and others; kindle their own fire, compass themselves with sparks, and walk in the light of their own fire, and of the sparks which they have kindled; and, in consequence, lie down in sorrow, having bidden adieu to the true meaning of a passage so very simple, taken in its connection, that one must wonder how it ever came to be misunderstood and misapplied. Those who wish to see more on this verse may consult Hammond, Whitby, Schoettgen, Rosenmuller, Pearce, Sir Norton Knatchbull, and Dodd.

To interpret this passage as the Calvinists do charges God with "respect of persons" and is a slander upon God's justice and His testimony of His own judgment and character. Let's look at another passage which has been misunderstood.

Eph 1:3 *Blessed be the God and Father of our Lord Jesus Christ, who hath blessed us with all spiritual blessings in heavenly places **in Christ:** 4 According as he hath chosen us **in him** before the foundation of the world, that we* *should be holy and without blame before him in love: 5 Having predestinated us unto the adoption of children by Jesus Christ to himself, according to the good pleasure of his will, 6 To the praise of the glory of his grace, wherein he hath made us accepted **in the beloved.** 7 In whom we have redemption through his blood, the forgiveness of sins, according to the riches of his grace; 8 Wherein he hath abounded toward us in all wisdom and prudence; 9 Having made known unto us the mystery of his will, according to his good pleasure which he hath purposed in himself: 10 That in the dispensation of the fulness of times he might gather together in one all things in Christ, both which are in heaven, and which are on earth; even in him: 11 In whom also we have obtained an inheritance, being predestinated according to the purpose of him who worketh all things after the counsel of his own will: 12 That we should be to the praise of his glory, who first trusted in Christ.*

Wow, that sounds like Calvinism, doesn't it? Yes, if people are ignorant of the apostle's subject and terms, it could easily confuse those who have already heard it used in that way. However, the careful and studied reader knows that the apostle is not speaking of individual's salvation, but of the privileges provided to those in a special people group called the church. The "us" and "we" refers to "us the Bride" and "we the Bride" not as individuals. Notice carefully verse 12 and its connection to verse 13 about the Gentiles being grafted into the vine – "we" and "ye" referring to people groups.

*Eph 1:12 That **we** should be to the praise of his glory, **who first trusted in Christ**. 13 In whom **ye also trusted**, **after that ye heard the word** of truth, the gospel of your salvation: in whom also **after that ye believed**, ye were sealed with that holy Spirit of promise,*

Paul is speaking of the privileges of coming into God's VESSEL OF MERCY – the CHURCH.   God's salvation plan from the beginning included the BRIDE of Christ and the blessings that would come upon this BRIDE.

Jesus **will have** a spotless BRIDE at the marriage supper of the Lamb; but the question is – **"Will you or even your church group be a part of it (2 Cor 11:1-4)?**   When I become a part of this Bride, then I can say, "US" and "We" concerning God's predetermination that "We be conformed to the image of Christ" or that He *"hath blessed us with all spiritual blessings in heavenly places in Christ: According as he hath chosen us in him before the foundation of the world, that we should be holy and without blame before him in love: Having predestinated us unto the adoption of children by Jesus Christ to himself, according to the good pleasure of his will, 6 To the praise of the glory of his grace, wherein he hath made us accepted in the beloved."*   This is all appropriate language for anyone who is presently a part of the Bride; but this language doesn't guarantee me to be a part, it just declares the blessings if I remain a part. This will be proven as we go along.

The privileged group will be there, but whether you will be a part of this privileged group is still dependant upon YOU hearing and believing to the end -- overcoming and being found faithful. As we said earlier, God having a privileged group doesn't ensure the salvation of the individuals unless they continue in the requirements and thus continue in the group in spirit and not just presence. The continuation and final victory of the group doesn't guarantee the continuation and victory of the individuals unless they stay in the group by meeting the necessary requirements.

God has designed the "Old Ship of Zion" to sail victoriously for the salvation of men; but will you get on? Will you stay on? That is the issue? The Bride will be pure and dressed in the righteousness of saints; but will you be of that number? Can you see the difference?

The churches of revelation were threatened with having their candlestick removed. Does this mean Jesus would not have a bride? NO, it means they would not be a part of it any more. The church members were separately charged with overcoming as individuals or having their names blotted out.

Listen to Paul throughout Ephesians and you will see the context of his words:

Eph 2:11 Wherefore remember, that ye being in time past Gentiles in the flesh, who are called Uncircumcision by that which is called the Circumcision in the flesh made by hands; 12 That at that time ye were without Christ, being aliens from the commonwealth of Israel, and strangers from the covenants of promise, having no hope, and without God in the world: 13 But now in Christ Jesus ye who sometimes were far off are made nigh by the blood of Christ. 14 For he is our peace, who hath made both one, *and hath broken down the middle wall of partition between us;*

The "ye" and "us" are obviously in the context of "believing Gentiles" and "believing Jews", not in the context of "you" and "me" simply as individuals. Paul is writing to a church concerning the privileges they now have entered into as one of God's churches. Ephesians 5:1-7 declares plainly that individuals are still in danger of falling back under God's wrath and only men with "deceitful vain words" would say otherwise. "Chosen in Christ" doesn't protect you as the individual from this reality.

Eph 5:1 Be ye therefore followers of God, as dear children; 2 And walk in love, as Christ also hath loved us, and hath given himself for us an offering and a sacrifice to God for a sweetsmelling savour. 3 But fornication, and all uncleanness, or covetousness, let it not be once named among you, as becometh saints; 4 Neither filthiness, nor foolish talking, nor jesting, which are not convenient: but rather giving of thanks. 5 For this ye know, that no whoremonger, nor unclean person, nor covetous man, who is an idolater, hath any inheritance in the kingdom of Christ and of God. 6 Let no man deceive you with vain words: for because of these things cometh the wrath of God upon the children of disobedience. 7 Be not ye therefore partakers with them.

Listen further:

Eph 2:18 For through him we both have access by one Spirit unto the Father. 19 Now therefore ye are no more strangers and foreigners, but fellowcitizens with the saints, and of the household of God; 20 And are built upon the foundation of the apostles and prophets, Jesus Christ himself being the chief corner stone; 21 In whom all the building fitly framed together

182

*groweth unto an holy temple in the Lord: 22 **In whom ye also are builded together for an habitation of God through the Spirit.***

The context is God's present administration of mercy containing both Jew and Gentile believers.

Eph 3:1 *¶ For this cause I Paul, the prisoner of Jesus Christ for **you Gentiles,** 2 If ye have heard of the dispensation of the grace of God which is given me **to you-ward:** 3 How that by revelation he made known unto me the mystery; (as I wrote afore in few words, 4 Whereby, when ye read, ye may understand my knowledge in the mystery of Christ) 5 Which in other ages was not made known unto the sons of men, as it is now revealed unto his holy apostles and prophets by the Spirit; 6 **That the Gentiles should be fellowheirs, and of the same body, and partakers of his promise in Christ by the gospel:***

Listen to the CONTEXT! If I joined the Marines I could declare that "WE are the greatest fighting force on the planet and WE have been chosen by God to protect human rights" or whatever; but that would only apply to me as a PART, and I could be kicked out or become a deserter. The group would still exist without me being a part; and the accolades would only cease to apply to me, not the group. Read Romans 11 and John 15 where individual "branches" can be severed, but the "root" still lives on with other branches. Let's continue looking at the context of Ephesians:

Eph 3:7 *Whereof I was made a minister, according to the gift of the grace of God given unto me by the effectual working of his power. 8 Unto me, who am less than the least of all saints, is this grace given, that I should preach among **the Gentiles** the* *unsearchable riches of Christ; 9 And to make all men see what is the fellowship of the mystery, **which from the beginning of the world hath been hid in God, who created all things by Jesus Christ:** 10 To the intent that now unto the principalities and powers in heavenly places **might be known by the church the manifold wisdom of God,** 11 **According to the eternal purpose which he purposed in Christ Jesus our Lord:.....5:25** Husbands, love your wives, even as **Christ also loved the church, and gave himself for it; 26 That he might sanctify and cleanse it with the washing of water by the word, 27 That he might present it to himself a glorious church, not having spot, or wrinkle, or any such thing; but that it should be holy and without blemish.** 28 So ought men to love their wives as their own bodies. He that loveth his wife loveth himself. 29 For no man ever yet hated his own flesh; but nourisheth and cherisheth it, **even as the Lord the church: 30 For we are members of his body, of his flesh, and of his bones.** 31 For this cause shall a man leave his father and mother, and shall be joined unto his wife, and they two shall be one flesh. 32 **This is a great mystery: but I speak concerning Christ and the church.***

All this is speaking of the PROGRAM, not the predestination of individual's salvation! Listen to James declare this explicitly:

Acts 15:14 *Simeon hath declared how God at the first did visit the **Gentiles, to take out of them a people** for his name. 15 And to this agree the words of the prophets; as it is written, 16 After this I will return, and will build again the tabernacle of David, which is fallen down; and I will build again the ruins thereof, and I will set it up: 17 That the residue of **men might seek after the Lord,** and **all the Gentiles, upon whom my name is called, saith the Lord, who doeth all these things. 18 Known unto God are all his works from the beginning of the world.** 19 Wherefore my sentence is, that we trouble not them, which from among the Gentiles are turned to God:*

Known unto God from the beginning is HIS PROGRAM, which included the open door to the Gentiles who wished to seek the Lord and be a part of His PEOPLE GROUP. The proper use of the term "foreknew" in this context is the word "envisioned". God has envisioned a BRIDE or REMNANT people group who meet certain criteria (II Co 6:17-7:1). This quality or character of people He has predestined to conform to the image of Christ through a process and program consistent with His holy and just nature (Ro 8:28-30). We will see that this people group whom God foreknew and determined to save is the BRIDE of Christ; but whether I as an individual will ultimately be a part of this group is still up to my choices.

God predestined a program and my responsibility is to get in the program and stay in the program if I wish to be saved by the program. Nothing in this passage is promoting Calvinistic "Respect of Persons" which God clearly denies and abhors.

Consider the following verses:

*De 4:20 But the LORD hath taken you, and brought you forth out of the iron furnace, even out of Egypt, to be unto **him a people** of inheritance, as ye are this day.*

*De 29:13 That he may establish thee to day **for a people unto himself**, and that he may be unto thee a God, as he hath said unto thee, and as he hath sworn unto thy fathers, to Abraham, to Isaac, and to Jacob.*

■ This is God's purpose for this people group

185

*De 32:21 They have moved me to jealousy with that which is not God; they have provoked me to anger with their vanities: and I will move **them to jealousy with those which are not a people;** I will provoke them to anger with a foolish nation.*

- This is God working with men who have free will. This is the preview and justification for the calling of the Gentiles.

*2Sa 7:24 For thou hast **confirmed to thyself thy people Israel to be a people unto thee for ever:** and thou, LORD, art become their God.*

*Ps 95:10 Forty years long was I grieved with this generation, and said, **It is a people** that do err in their heart, and they have not known my ways:*

*Jer 13:11 For as the girdle cleaveth to the loins of a man, so have I caused to cleave unto me the **whole house of Israel and the whole house of Judah**, saith the LORD; **that they might be unto me for a people, and for a name, and for a praise, and for a glory: <u>but they would not hear.</u>***

- God's purpose is hindered by free will. This doesn't determine the salvation or damnation of all the people in the group as we are not speaking of individuals, but God's dealing with a group.

*1Pe 2:10 Which in time past were not a people, **but are now the people of God:** which **had not obtained mercy,** but **now have obtained mercy.***

- Now we see the Church as the privileged group (vessels of mercy) whom God has chosen to provoke Israel to jealousy and possibly save **some** of them yet (Romans 11:11-14).

Listen to a very clear passage which presents both the predetermination of a program and the free-will actions of the individuals within.

Acts 17:23 *For as I passed by, and beheld your devotions, I found an altar with this inscription, TO THE UNKNOWN GOD. Whom therefore ye ignorantly worship, him declare I unto you. 24 God that made the world and all things therein, seeing that he is Lord of heaven and earth, dwelleth not in temples made with hands; 25 Neither is worshipped with men's hands, as though he needed any thing, seeing he giveth to all life, and breath, and all things; 26* **And hath made of one blood all nations of men for to dwell on all the face of the earth, and hath determined the times before appointed, and the bounds of their habitation;** *{*PREDETERMINED*} 27 That* **they should seek the Lord, if haply they might feel after him, and find him,** *{*NOT PREDETERMINED*} though he be not far from every one of us:*

Nothing could be clearer to the honest and unbiased reader. God's Word is perfectly consistent and never contradicts itself. God is no respecter of persons; never showed partiality or favoritism; and is not a deceiver or a hypocrite. We don't know what God knows or doesn't know of man's future choices and actions; but He can only know that whatever a man does, he does without God showing partiality to him. There are a number of Scriptures that clearly indicate that God doesn't know all that individuals will do and choose. Here are a few.

Ge 2:19 *And out of the ground the LORD God formed every beast of the field, and every fowl of the air; and brought them* unto Adam *to see what he would call them*: and whatsoever Adam called every living creature, that was the name thereof.

Gen 6 " And GOD saw that the wickedness of man was great in the earth, and that every imagination of the thoughts of his heart was only evil continually. **And it repented the LORD that he had made man on the earth**, and it grieved him at his heart. And the LORD said, I will destroy man whom I have created from the face of the earth; both man, and beast, and the creeping thing, and the fowls of the air; for it repenteth me that I have made

Ge 18:21 I will go down now, and see whether they have done altogether according to the cry of it, **which is come unto me; and if not, <u>I will know</u>.**

Ge 22:12 And he said, Lay not thine hand upon the lad, neither do thou any thing unto him: **for <u>now I know</u> that thou fearest God**, seeing thou hast not withheld thy son, thine only son from me.

Ex 16:4 Then said the LORD unto Moses, Behold, I will rain bread from heaven for you; and the people shall go out and gather a certain rate every day, **that I may prove them, whether they will walk in my law, or no**.

De 8:2 And thou shalt remember all the way which the LORD thy God led thee these forty years in the wilderness, to humble thee, and to prove thee, **to know what was in thine heart, whether thou wouldest keep his commandments, or no.**

I Sam 15:11 It repenteth me that I have set up Saul to be king: for he is turned back from following me, and hath not performed my commandments.

1Sa 15:35 *And Samuel came no more to see Saul until the day of his death: nevertheless Samuel mourned for Saul: and* **the LORD repented that he had made Saul king over Israel.**

2Ch 32:31 *Howbeit in the business of the ambassadors of the princes of Babylon, who sent unto him to enquire of the wonder that was done in the land, God left him, to try him,* ***that he might know all that was in his heart****.*

These passages are God's Word and **choice of words** and are NOT meant to deceive, but rather to reveal the truth of God. The WORD is God's revelation of Himself to man. It would be hypocritical and deceptive for God to say these things if they really were not true. If we speculate beyond what the Bible actually says, then we move into the realm of **imagination, not revelation. We don't know for sure what God foresees or doesn't foresee.** It is **sure** that God knows what HE will do in His program; but whether He knows all that men will do and who will ultimately be saved is uncertain if we limit our speculations to the realms of God's own revelation of Himself. To deny this is false piety rearing its ugly head, not a true love of God.

But what about **Mt 25:34?** *"Then shall the King say unto them on his right hand, Come, ye blessed of my Father, inherit the* ***kingdom prepared*** *for you* ***from the foundation of the world"***

Does that teach that our inheritance was all done from the foundation of the world? Listen to some similar expressions

Lu 11:50 That the blood of all the prophets, which was shed **from the foundation of the world,** may be required of this generation;

Lu 1:70 As he spake by the mouth of his holy prophets, which have been **since the world began:**

Ac 3:21 Whom the heaven must receive until the times of restitution of all things, which God hath spoken by the mouth of all his holy prophets **since the world began.**

Do these verses say that the prophets were all martyred at the beginning of the world or that all the prophets prophesied at the beginning of the world? NO. It is simply saying this PROGRAM and PROCESS has been going on since that time. Jesus told his disciples "I go to prepare a place for you". Was this true or was it already done? The same language with the same meaning is being used in this verse:

Re 17:8 The beast that thou sawest was, and is not; and shall ascend out of the bottomless pit, and go into perdition: and they that dwell on the earth shall wonder, **whose names were not written in the book of life from the foundation of the world,** when they behold the beast that was, and is not, and yet is.

Names were being put in and blotted out since the beginning of the world when men began making choices to be faithful or unfaithful to God's salvation program. Consider again how God uses expressions in the comparison of the next three verses.

Re 13:8 And all that dwell upon the earth shall worship him, whose names are not written in the book of life of **the Lamb slain from the foundation of the world.**

Heb 9:26 *For then must he often have* **suffered since the foundation of the world**: *but* **now once in the end of the world hath he appeared to put away sin by the sacrifice of himself.**

1Pe 1:20 *Who verily was* **foreordained before the foundation of the world**, *but was* **manifest in these last times for you**,

When did Jesus suffer? The obvious conclusion is that, though the plan and program was from the beginning, the suffering wasn't until it actually happened "in the end" or latter part of the world's existence. We must never put on God's expressions more than was intended. Gethsemane was not just a show; but a real struggle for Jesus to continue faithful to the end and overcome. Don't run to the mysterious when there is a logical and practical explanation which fits clearly with what the whole counsel of God teaches. Those who run to the mysterious interpretations are just trying to avoid conviction and personal responsibility. They are feverishly trying to preserve their "security" in Christ; but are only "saving their life" which will cause them to "lose it" (Mk 8:34-38).

Regardless of what God knows, doesn't know, foresees, doesn't foresee, plans or doesn't plan; He has clearly told us that with Him THERE IS NO RESPECT OF PERSONS. In the matter of election we are clearly told that we have a responsibility to "make our calling and election sure". How does the Calvinist explain this? How could this fit with their false concepts of "foreknowledge" and "election"?

191

2Pe 1:10 *Wherefore the rather, brethren, give diligence to make your calling and election sure: for **if ye do** these things, ye shall never fall:*

We are told that individuals who were once elect in an elect people group were cut off due to unbelief and could later be grafted in again if they repented and believed on Christ – **Romans 11:13-23**. God's program is certain, but my place in the program rests upon my daily faithfulness to the conditions God has set. One passage which speaks of God's program and His faithfulness in it is often misused to teach "respect of persons".

Rom 8:28 *And we know that all things work together for good to them that love God, to them who are the called according to his purpose. 29 For whom he did foreknow, he also did predestinate to be conformed to the image of his Son, that he might be the firstborn among many brethren. 30 Moreover whom he did predestinate, them he also called: and whom he called, them he also justified: and whom he justified, them he also glorified. 31 What shall we then say to these things? If God be for us, who can be against us?*

This passage speaks clearly that God will follow through faithfully; but it doesn't contradict or change all the other passages which clearly teach that whether or not I have a part in this wonderful program is dependent upon my continuing in it. It can be easily proved from the same letter to the Romans that this "Goodness of God" is striving to lead men to repentance who can definitely resist (Ro 2:3-11); and this same "Goodness of God" must be continued in lest the one's in it be cut off from it (Ro 11:22). Who can deny that this "Goodness of God" is the same program Paul is speaking of in Romans 8:28-30? No intelligent person can deny this fact. The "Goodness of God" leading men to repentance is for this very program of conforming them to the image of Christ; and those cut off from the "Goodness of God" in Romans 11:17-23 WERE IN this program already and ceased to be – but could actually get back in under certain conditions. Who can deny this?

Romans 8:28-30 does not declare the opposite of 2 Peter 1:10 above. It actually says nothing about a guarantee for me; but only that God will follow through faithfully on His end of the deal. It is the same as God saying, "I will never leave thee, nor forsake thee"; but we know that we can leave and forsake Him. We have proved back in Chapter 8 that many Scriptures clearly teach the possibility of men, who were once on their way to heaven, being lost and going to Hell. The warnings to "hold fast" and "continue in the faith" are everywhere throughout the Scriptures. Only willful ignorance would deny what we have clearly proven from the Word of God.

You say, "Yes, but what about John 6:39?" *"And this is the Father's will which hath sent me, that of all which he hath given me I should lose nothing, but should raise it up again at the last day"*

Let Jesus interpret His own meaning in John 17:12 *"While I was with them in the world, I kept them in thy name: those that thou gavest me I have kept, and none of them is lost, but the son of perdition; that the scripture might be fulfilled."* Who is he obviously referring to? He is speaking of His ministry among His apostles. Listen a few verses later: "*15 I pray not that thou shouldest take them* **(the apostles)** *out of the world, but that thou shouldest keep them from the evil. 16 They are not of the world, even as I am not of the world. 17 Sanctify them through thy truth: thy word is truth. 18 As thou hast sent me into the world, even so have I also sent them into the world. 19 And for their sakes I sanctify myself, that they also might be sanctified through the truth.   20* **Neither pray I for these (apostles)** *alone, but for them also which shall believe on me through their word;"*

It is more than obvious that Jesus is speaking of the apostle's free will, their danger of falling, and His ministry to establish them in the faith. He also prays for those who will be converted through the ministry of these apostles – all Christians. Nothing is spoken here of some "eternal security" or special election which removes the necessity of enduring to the end; but actually underscores that necessity.

If God had "elect" individuals whom He chose to save before they were even born, then He would never call anyone else whom He knew would not accept the call – for this would be hypocrisy and mockery on God's part. But we see many instances where God called those who didn't respond properly. How could God only call those whom He foreknew would respond? His foreknowledge would only be that they were the only one's called, so how would He foresee that the other's would not respond to the call that never happened??? Those who teach such nonsense are simply too shallow minded to think it through to the logical absurdity. Ask them if prayer really changes anything. Whatever God knows, we can be sure He knows that the salvation or damnation of men did not rest in any sense upon Him showing respect of persons or favoritism. Foreknowledge cannot change the future or it is not foreknowledge at all.

The Bible warnings are **not** saying to "make sure you really got it" but rather to "hold fast what you have" (Heb 3:12-14). If someone only has a "superficial" faith as some charge upon those who fall away, then they actually never fell away! Falling away from a superficial faith is a **good thing**; and telling these people to hold fast *what they had* would then be a **bad thing**. Just because the apostles said that certain false teachers left the church because they were really imposters from the start anyway (I John 2:19), does not mean this is the scenario every time someone falls away. This is sloppy Bible exegesis to an extreme. We have proved the opposite already for those with ears to hear.

Every man must be able to say at the end of his journey, *"2Ti 4:7 I have fought a good fight, I have finished my course, I have kept the faith: 8 Henceforth there is laid up for me a crown of righteousness, which the Lord, the righteous [IMPARTIAL] judge, shall give me at that day:"* ...Or else he will be lost, because this type of person is the only product the Bride, Vine, Shepherd, etc. will produce, and it is up to you if you ultimately end up being the "precious fruit of the earth" or not. Paul concluded his statement thus: *"...and not to me only, but unto all them also that love his appearing."* The crown of righteousness is being

195

crowned as the "righteous" just like the "crown of life" is being crowned with "life eternal". This is given without respect of persons to those who run their race with patience like Romans 2 and Hebrews 12 speak of.

Lovers of truth and righteousness have no problem seeing the truth when it is presented to them; but those with an ax to grind or sin to hide will never come to the truth until they repent of their self will. I say this confidently not only because the Bible clearly teaches it; but because I was raised in error through growing up in church, going to Bible Colleges, and in preaching the error as a associate pastor and as a pastor in the Baptist Denomination - YET because I was willing to "hear" and "learn" of the Father, He led me out of that error. I didn't have books like this to explain it all to me either. I know that my willingness to exercise "self-abandoning honesty" was a key to being able to understand truth and walk in it. It is the same for all men – **FOR THERE IS NO RESPECT OF PERSONS WITH GOD.**

For Free Counseling:

Living Faith Christian Fellowship
27216 Ingel Rd, Brookfield, MO 64628
Pastor Mark Bullen
660-258-2201
www.thefaithoncedelivered.info

This title is also available in Audiobook format.

Look for this and other titles from
Open Vision Media
at your favorite audiobook retailers
and ATPublishers.com

Made in the USA
Lexington, KY
06 March 2017